Luke 2V21
Luke 2V39 ¢40 - 52

Hope in
HURTFUL TIMES

A Study of 1 Peter

BIBLE STUDY GUIDE

From the Bible-teaching ministry of

Charles R. Swindoll

INSIGHT FOR LIVING

Chuck graduated in 1963 from Dallas Theological Seminary, where he now serves as the school's fourth president, helping to prepare a new generation of men and women for the ministry. Chuck has served in pastorates in three states: Massachusetts, Texas, and California, including almost twenty-three years at the First Evangelical Free Church in Fullerton, California. His sermon messages have been aired over radio since 1979 as the *Insight for Living* broadcast. A best-selling author, Chuck has written numerous books and booklets on many subjects.

Based on the outlines and transcripts of Chuck's sermons, the study guide text is co-authored by Ken Gire, a graduate of Texas Christian University and Dallas Theological Seminary. He also wrote the Living Insights sections.

Editor in Chief: Cynthia Swindoll	**Production Artist:** Gary Lett
Coauthor of Text: Ken Gire	**Typographer:** Bob Haskins
Assistant Editor: Wendy Peterson	**Director, Communications Division:** Deedee Snyder
Copy Editing Supervisor: Marty Anderson	**Project Manager:** Alene Cooper
Copy Editor: Connie Laser	**Print Production Manager:** Deedee Snyder
Designer: Diana Vasquez	**Assistant Production Manager:** John Norton

Unless otherwise identified, all Scripture references are from the New American Standard Bible, © The Lockman Foundation 1960, 1962, 1963, 1968, 1971, 1972, 1973, 1975, 1977. Used by permission. The other translations cited are *The Living Bible* [LB], and *The New Testament in Modern English* [PHILLIPS].

An effort has been made to locate sources and obtain permission where necessary for the quotations used in this book. In the event of any unintentional omission, a modification will gladly be incorporated in future printings.

ISBN 0-8499-6235-8

Printed in the United States of America

COVER DESIGN: Nina Paris

COVER PAINTING: *Peter's Denial* by Carl Bloch. Used by permission of Frederiksborg Museum, Hillerod, Denmark.

CONTENTS

INTRODUCTION

I find it interesting that Peter, as a disciple of Christ, is clearly the most popular of the twelve . . . yet Peter, as a writer of Scripture, is not nearly as well known.

Too bad. His first letter offers wonderful hope to people who live in hurtful times. Without denying the reality of pain, he sets forth dynamic and trustworthy counsel that anyone—in any generation—would find reassuring.

Few individuals lived in tougher times. Christians were hated, mistreated, and driven from their homes. Martyrdom commonly occurred. Madman Nero was the ruler of the known world, and we don't need a rehearsal of his evil, corrupt reign. But whatever the hour, Christ is Lord. He has everything under control. And the old fisherman-turned-apostle provides confident counsel for all to believe.

May these studies be more than a little helpful. My desire is that they will turn your whole mind-set toward our Lord and His will, regardless of the circumstances in which you find yourself these days.

Chuck Swindoll

Chuck Swindoll

PUTTING TRUTH
INTO ACTION

K nowledge apart from application falls short of God's desire for
His children. He wants us to apply what we learn so that we
will change and grow. This study guide was prepared with these
goals in mind. As you go through the following pages, we hope your
desire to discover biblical truth will grow as your understanding of
God's Word increases and that you will be encouraged to apply what
you've learned.

To assist you in your study, we've included a section called
Living Insights at the end of each lesson. These exercises will
challenge you to study further and to think of specific ways to
put your discoveries into action.

There are many ways to use this guide—in personal devotions,
group studies, discussions with friends and family, and Sunday school
classes. And, of course, it's an ideal study aid when you're listening
to its corresponding *Insight for Living* radio series.

To benefit most from this study guide, we would encourage you
to consider it a spiritual journal. That's why we've included space
in the Living Insights for recording your thoughts and discoveries.
We hope you'll return to those sections often for review and encouragement as you continue to grow in your walk with Christ.

Ken Gire

Ken Gire
Coauthor of Text
Author of Living Insights

Hope in
HURTFUL TIMES

A Study of 1 Peter

Chapter 1

PETER: THE MAN AND HIS MESSAGE

Survey of 1 Peter

Of all the disciples, none stands as front and center as Peter. Whether he's sloshing around in a sinking boat weighted with fish or swinging a sword in a torchlit garden, Peter dominates every scene he's in.

Alexander Whyte speaks of this disciple's pervasive presence and influence.

> After the name of our Lord Himself, no name comes up so often in the Four Gospels as Peter's name. No disciple speaks so often and so much as Peter. Our Lord speaks oftener to Peter than to any other of His disciples; sometimes in blame and sometimes in praise. No disciple is so pointedly reproved by our Lord as Peter, and no disciple ever ventures to reprove his Master but Peter. No other disciple ever so boldly confessed and outspokenly acknowledged and encouraged our Lord as Peter repeatedly did; and no one ever intruded, and interfered, and tempted Him as Peter repeatedly did also. His Master spoke words of approval, and praise, and even blessing to Peter the like of which He never spoke to any other man. And at the same time, and almost in the same breath, He said harder things to Peter than He ever said to any other of His twelve disciples, unless it was to Judas.[1]

---

1. Alexander Whyte, *Bible Characters from the New Testament* (reprint, New Canaan, Conn.: Keats Publishing, 1981), vol. 1, p. 46.

Before we begin a study of Peter's first letter, let's turn back to the Gospels and make a brief sketch of his life, looking at the lines and shadings that composed his personality and destiny.

Brief Sketch of Peter's Life

A brief pencil sketch will detail enough of the four main areas of Peter's life so that we can glimpse some of the thoughts and feelings that undoubtedly went into his letter.

His Calling

We first catch sight of Peter in Mark 1:16–18. Out in their sun-blanched boat, he and his brother Andrew are heaving a hopeful net into the blue-gray waters of the Sea of Galilee. They are partners in a lucrative fishing business, along with James and John (see also Luke 5:3–11). All this changes, however, when Jesus' voice calls out to them from the bustling shore.

> And as He was going along by the Sea of Galilee, He saw Simon and Andrew, the brother of Simon, casting a net in the sea; for they were fishermen. And Jesus said to them, "Follow Me, and I will make you become fishers of men." And they immediately left the nets and followed Him.

No hesitation, no scrambling to secure possessions, no backward glances. Jesus called; Peter followed.

To help us understand this remarkable response, William Barclay explains some of the nuances of Peter's nature.

> Peter was a Galilean, and a typical Galilean. Josephus was for a time governor of Galilee and he knew the Galileans well. He says of them: "They were ever fond of innovations, and by nature disposed to changes. . . . They were ever ready to follow a leader and to begin an insurrection." He goes on to say that they were notoriously quick in temper and given to quarreling, but that withal they were the most chivalrous of men. "The Galilaeans have never been destitute of courage." . . . The Talmud says of the Galileans: "They were ever more anxious for honour than for gain." Quick-tempered, impulsive, emotional, easily roused by an appeal to adventure, loyal

to the end—Peter was a typical man of Galilee.[2]

His Role

It wasn't long until this Galilean fisherman rose to a position of leadership among the disciples. In Matthew 10:2, Peter is referred to as "the first" among the Twelve. The Greek word is *protos*, which can mean not only first in order but chief or first in prominence. In other passages we learn that he was also a spokesman for the disciples—he was the one who was bold enough to ask Jesus questions and nervy enough to insist on explanations (see Matt. 18:21; 19:27). And when he wasn't asking questions himself, he was fielding them from those outside the group as Jesus' representative (see 17:24).

Peter was also the primary one who answered the often penetrating questions Jesus posed to the disciples—like this one in Matthew 16.

> Now when Jesus came into the district of Caesarea Philippi, He began asking His disciples, saying, "Who do people say that the Son of Man is?" And they said, "Some say John the Baptist; and others, Elijah; but still others, Jeremiah, or one of the prophets." He said to them, "But who do you say that I am?" And Simon Peter answered and said, "Thou art the Christ, the Son of the living God." (vv. 13–16)

The "you" in Jesus' second question is plural, addressed to the whole group. Yet Peter was the one who stepped forward with an answer. And as a result of Peter's faith, Jesus blessed him and changed his name from Simon to Peter, meaning "rock."

Not all was blessing and praise, however. Peter also had the dubious role of being the most rebuked of Jesus' disciples, especially when his Galilean impulsiveness merged with his heartfelt loyalty (see vv. 21–23). Even Peter's loyalty, though, would crumble under the weight of the Cross.

His Denial

If you were to graph Peter's life like a chart of the Dow-Jones industrials, there would be extreme highs and lows. If the highest point was Peter's experience with Christ on the Mount of

2. William Barclay, *The Master's Men* (New York, N.Y.: Abingdon Press, 1959), p. 18.

Transfiguration, his denial in the temple courtyard would be tantamount to the stock market crash of 1929. Jesus predicted Peter's crash in His final board meeting with His disciples in the Upper Room. But Peter, still impulsive in his loyalty, vowed that he would die before he would deny his Lord (see Mark 14:27–31).

In spite of Peter's insistence, however, his stock plummeted in the wee hours of that cold, dark morning. He denied his Lord not once, but three times, just as Jesus had said he would.

> And as Peter was below in the courtyard, one of the servant-girls of the high priest came, and seeing Peter warming himself, she looked at him, and said, "You, too, were with Jesus the Nazarene." But he denied it, saying, "I neither know nor understand what you are talking about." And he went out onto the porch. And the maid saw him, and began once more to say to the bystanders, "This is one of them!" But again he was denying it. And after a little while the bystanders were again saying to Peter, "Surely you are one of them, for you are a Galilean too." But he began to curse and swear, "I do not know this man you are talking about!" And immediately a cock crowed a second time. And Peter remembered how Jesus had made the remark to him, "Before a cock crows twice, you will deny Me three times." And he began to weep. (vv. 66–72)

When that kind of crash occurs in your life, it ushers in a period of great depression. With it comes a gloom and pall that settles darkly over you. The failure seems so devastating that you feel you're through forever, that you've abdicated all possibilities of ever holding a leadership position again. But the restoration Jesus gave Peter should give you a bullish outlook on the record lows in your own portfolio.

His Leadership

The words that forecast a turnaround in Peter's stock are found, appropriately, at the Resurrection site. There the angel told the women who came to anoint Jesus' body that He had risen and that they must go and "tell His disciples *and Peter*" the good news (16:7, emphasis added). Two little words—"and Peter"—indicate that Peter's stock is on the upswing.

4

Those who know these types of things say that the Gospel of Mark is really the transcribed notes and dictated thoughts of Peter. If this is true, then it was Peter himself who included these two words! And if these really are his words, I can't help but imagine that the old fisherman had to brush away a tear and swallow a lump when he got to this point in the story.[3]

The actual turnaround comes in John 21. Peter was fishing when the words of Jesus came to him from the shore, jostling a sleeping memory. He immediately "threw himself into the sea" in a rush to get to his Lord (v. 7). Once on shore, Peter found breakfast waiting for him and the other disciples—Jesus Himself tending to their needs. While they were all hunched around the campfire, Jesus took Peter aside and began his restoration.

Three times He asked Peter if he loved Him, providing this devastated disciple a chance to reconfirm his love for each of the times he had denied it. And with the words "Tend My lambs . . . Shepherd My sheep . . . Tend My sheep," Jesus reestablished Peter's role of leadership in His kingdom and then sealed it with the command to follow Him (vv. 15–22).

A quick look at Luke's record will show how this second chance turned Peter's life around.

It was Peter who took the lead in choosing a disciple to take Judas' place (Acts 1). It was Peter who became spokesman for the first evangelistic outreach at Pentecost (chap. 2). It was Peter who, with John, healed the lame man at the temple (chap. 3). It was Peter who defied the Sanhedrin, refusing to be silent about Jesus (chap. 4). It was Peter who presided over the grim task of dealing with Ananias and Sapphira (chap. 5). It was Peter who dealt decisively with the deceit of Simon the magician (chap. 8). It was Peter who reached out to Cornelius, a Gentile, after God revealed to him that the gospel would be extended universally (10:1–11:18).

And this was the man God used to pen the two letters known as 1 and 2 Peter. He was a man who could identify with failure . . . who could understand pain . . . who was well acquainted with suffering.

---

3. Max Lucado, *No Wonder They Call Him the Savior* (Portland, Oreg.: Multnomah Press, 1986), p. 95.

General Survey of Peter's Letter

The chart at the end of this lesson gives a bird's-eye view of 1 Peter, but here are the pertinent compass settings you need to get your bearings before unfolding chapter one.

The Recipients

First Peter 1:1–2 identifies the sender of the letter as Peter and tells us that the recipients were "those who reside as aliens, scattered throughout Pontus, Galatia, Cappadocia, Asia, and Bithynia, who are chosen according to the foreknowledge of God the Father."

In his commentary James Moffatt discusses the setting that these recipients found themselves in.

> This beautiful epistle is addressed to Christians in Asia Minor who needed heartening and encouragement under the strain of a persecution-period. It was a time of tension, due to interference by the State authorities, who had obviously become suspicious of the Christian movement as immoral and treasonable. This set up, in some circles of the church, a feeling of perplexity and hesitation. Christians were suffering from the unwelcome attentions of Government officials, as well as from social annoyances, and they required to be rallied. The purpose of Peter is to recall them to the resources of their faith. Hence the emphasis upon hope.[4]

The Theme

There are only 105 verses in this letter, but the theme of suffering surfaces time and time again.

> In this you greatly rejoice, even though now for a little while, if necessary, you have been distressed by various trials. (1:6)

> Beloved, do not be surprised at the fiery ordeal among you, which comes upon you for your testing, as though some strange thing were happening to

---

4. James Moffatt, The General Epistles: James, Peter, and Judas (London, England: Hodder and Stoughton, 1928), p. 85.

you; but to the degree that you share the sufferings of Christ, keep on rejoicing; so that also at the revelation of His glory, you may rejoice with exultation. (4:12–13).

Be of sober spirit, be on the alert. Your adversary, the devil, prowls about like a roaring lion, seeking someone to devour. But resist him, firm in your faith, knowing that the same experiences of suffering are being accomplished by your brethren who are in the world. And after you have suffered for a little while, the God of all grace, who called you to His eternal glory in Christ, will Himself perfect, confirm, strengthen and establish you. (5:8–10)

The Purpose

Peter's purpose is to remind Christians that painful times are not an end in themselves and that there is hope in spite of suffering. An echo of that thought is resonated by contemporary author M. Scott Peck.

It is in this whole process of meeting and solving problems that life has its meaning. Problems are the cutting edge that distinguishes between success and failure. Problems call forth our courage and our wisdom. . . . When we desire to encourage the growth of the human spirit, we challenge and encourage the human capacity to solve problems, just as in school we deliberately set problems for our children to solve. It is through the pain of confronting and resolving problems that we learn. As Benjamin Franklin said, "Those things that hurt, instruct."[5]

Lessons to Be Learned from Peter's Model

Three come to mind. First: *Failure in the past does not nullify purpose in the future*. It's easy to convince yourself that once you've stumbled and fallen on your face you're fated to spend the rest of your days on the ground, staring at the dirt. Why? Because the most

5. M. Scott Peck, The Road Less Traveled (New York, N.Y.: Simon and Schuster, A Touchstone Book, 1978), p. 16.

difficult person to forgive is yourself. But Peter's example shows you how to grasp the hand that reaches down to pick you up . . . and how to dust yourself off and get on with your life (see Ps. 51:1–13).

Second: *A broken heart is great preparation for healing fractured lives.* Stop and think about it. When you are hurting, who touches you more profoundly and more permanently—the one who has been sheltered or the one who has been shattered (see 2 Cor. 1:3–4)?

Third: *One letter of hope brings more encouragement than a thousand thoughts never expressed.* A final thing we learn from Peter's life is the importance of expressing encouragement. Peter didn't just pray for those who suffered, he wrote to them as well. And the words fell on their parched hearts like cool water (see Prov. 25:25).

> —Following the Living Insights section, you will find a chart
> that provides a helpful overview of 1 Peter.

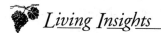 ## Living Insights STUDY ONE

Take the lessons you learned from Peter's life and try them on for size. Tailor-make them to fit around the contours of your own life by answering the following questions.

- Is there a major failure hanging in your closet that haunts you to this day? If so, bring it out into the light and describe it.

_____

_____

_____

_____

Do you feel that it has nullified your purpose in the future? Why?

_____

_____

_____

What does the Bible say about past sins that have been repented of?

Psalm 32:5 _____

Isaiah 1:18 _____

Psalm 103:11–12 _____

Isaiah 44:22 _____

1 John 1:9 _____

- Was your heart broken as a result of that failure? If so, describe how you felt.

_____

_____

_____

_____

What does the Bible say regarding a broken heart?

Psalm 34:18 _____

Psalm 51:17 _____

Psalm 147:3 _____

Has your brokenness helped you in healing the fractured lives of others? How?

_____

_____

_____

_____

_____

- Describe a letter you received this past year that brought you encouragement.

_____

_____

_____

_____

_____

When was the last time you wrote a letter to encourage someone who desperately needed to hear those words?

_____

_____

Take a few minutes to pray for God's Spirit to reveal someone you know who is hurting and in need of encouragement. Now take a few minutes to write that person a letter of hope, won't you?

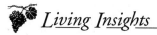 *Living Insights* _____

Let's take some time now to reflect on Peter's life and your own. You might want to use the following prayer as a catalyst to some specific petitions and praises of your own.

Dear Lord Jesus,

Thank you for Peter. He was a great man. He loved you so much. He left everything to follow you. In your name he healed the sick, cast out demons, and preached the kingdom. For three and a half faithful years he stood beside you. And when the soldiers came to take you away, he stood up for you. When the others deserted you, he followed all the way to the temple courtyard.

I confess I would have never made it that far.

Help me not to pass judgment on him, Lord. Rather, may his great and fervent love for you pass judgment on me.

Help me to see that I deny you in so many areas of my life, in so many ways and at so many different times.

When I am too busy to pray, I deny that you are the center of my life.

When I neglect your Word, I deny that you are competent to guide me.

When I worry, I deny that you are Lord of my circumstances.

When I turn my head from the hungry and the homeless, I deny that you are a God of mercy who has put me here to be your hands and your feet.

When I steal something from another person to enrich or enhance my life—whether that be something material or some credit that is rightly due another, which I have claimed for myself—I deny you are the source of all blessings.

Forgive me, Jesus, for all those quiet ways, known only to you, in which I have denied you . . . .

Thank you for all the times you have prayed for me that my faith might not fail. There is no telling how many times I have been rescued from Satan's hand because you stood beside me. And thank you, most faithful of friends, that no matter how terribly I have failed you, I can always look into your eyes, and there find forgiveness.[6]

6. Ken Gire, *Intimate Moments with the Savior* (Grand Rapids, Mich.: Zondervan Publishing House, Daybreak Books, 1989), pp. 103–4.

SURVEY OF 1 PETER

Major message: Stand firm in the true grace of God! (5:12) **Goal:** To give hope and encouragement to all who hurt.
Date: About A.D. 63. **Recipients:** Christians who were scattered, persecuted, and maligned.

	Our Living Hope	Our Strange Life	Our Fiery Ordeal	
Introduction	"*May grace and peace be yours . . .*" (1:2)	"*Beloved, I urge you . . .*" (2:11)	"*Beloved, do not be surprised . . .*" (4:12)	**Conclusion**
	as we claim our hope. (1:3–12)	abstain! (2:11–12)	Don't be surprised. (4:12)	
	as we walk in holiness. (1:13–25)	submit! (2:13–7)	Keep on rejoicing. (4:13)	
	as we grow in Christ. (2:1–10)	be humble! (3:8–22)	Entrust your soul (4:19)	
		arm yourselves! (4:1–6)		
		glorify God! (4:7–11)	Cast your anxiety. (5:7)	
1:1	1:2–2:10	2:11–4:11	4:12–5:13	5:14
Emphasis	Informing	Exhorting	Comforting	
Grace	. . . to go on	. . . to stand firm	. . . to rejoice	
Hope	A *living* hope through Christ's resurrection (1:3)	A *calm* hope through personal submission (3:6)	A *firm* hope through faith (4:19)	

Chapter 2

HOW WE CAN SMILE
THROUGH SUFFERING
1 Peter 1:1–12

We all exhibit different characteristics. We don't look alike. We don't act alike. We don't dress alike. We have different tastes in food, in music, and in the books we read. We have dissimilar backgrounds, goals, and motivations. We have different philosophies, politics, and religions. Our weights vary. Our heights vary. So does the color of our skin.

But there is one thing we all have in common; we all know what it means to hurt.

Suffering is a universal language. Tears are the same for Jews or Christians or Muslims, for white people or black people or brown, for children or adults or the elderly.

Since pain is such a pervasive problem, we need a potent prescription. Peter's first epistle dispenses that prescription with advice that tells us how we can smile through suffering. But before we get into our text for today, let's take a few minutes to review.

A Brief Reminder

The writer of 1 Peter was a man well acquainted with suffering. He suffered a broken heart when he denied Jesus on the night of His betrayal (see Matt. 26:75). The people Peter wrote to were displaced believers who were being singed by the flames of persecution. Their circumstances were the bleakest imaginable. Yet Peter didn't try to pump them up with positive thinking. Instead, he gently touched his hand to their chins and lifted their faces skyward—so they could see beyond their circumstances to their celestial calling.

> Peter, an apostle of Jesus Christ, to those who reside as aliens, scattered throughout Pontus, Galatia, Cappadocia, Asia, and Bithynia, who are chosen according to the foreknowledge of God the Father, by the sanctifying work of the Spirit, that you may obey Jesus Christ and be sprinkled with His blood:

May grace and peace be yours in fullest measure.
(1 Pet. 1:1–2)

Peter attempts to put pain in perspective by focusing on our position in Christ. We are chosen. We are being sanctified. And we have a full measure of God's grace and peace available to us. Those truths form the skeleton of strong doctrine. But without being fleshed out, they are hard and bony and difficult to embrace. Knowing that, Peter reminds his readers of all they have to cling to.

Regarding Suffering: Why Christians Can Rejoice

James tells us to "consider it all joy, my brethren, when you encounter various trials" (1:2). Underscore "my brethren," for there is no reason to rejoice in suffering if a person isn't a Christian. What reasons do Christians have for rejoicing? There are at least six.

We Have a Living Hope

Blessed be the God and Father of our Lord Jesus Christ, who according to His great mercy has caused us to be born again to a living hope through the resurrection of Jesus Christ from the dead. (v. 3)

As difficult to read as some pages of your life may be, nothing that occurs to you on this earth falls into the category of a final chapter. Your final chapter is heaven. And your final meeting is not with the antagonist in your life's story but with the author Himself. Also, this hope that we have is a living one, based on the resurrection of Christ. If God brought Jesus through the most painful of trials and from the pit of death itself, certainly He can bring us through whatever we face.

We Have a Permanent Inheritance

To obtain an inheritance which is imperishable and undefiled and will not fade away, reserved in heaven for you. (v. 4)

Our ultimate home is heaven. And our place there is reserved under the constant, omnipotent surveillance of almighty God. Nothing can destroy it, defile it, diminish it, or displace it.

We Have Divine Protection

Who are protected by the power of God through

14

faith for a salvation ready to be revealed in the last time. (v. 5)

Under heaven's lock and key, we are protected by the most efficient security system available—the power of God. There is no way that we will be lost in the process of suffering, no matter how chronic or acute the pain may be. No disorder, no disease, not even death itself can steal away God's ultimate protection over our lives.

We Have a Developing Faith

> In this you greatly rejoice, even though now for a little while, if necessary, you have been distressed by various trials, that the proof of your faith, being more precious than gold which is perishable, even though tested by fire, may be found to result in praise and glory and honor at the revelation of Jesus Christ. (vv. 6–7)

Here is the first of several references in Peter's letter to rejoicing. The words "even though" indicate that the joy is unconditional and does not depend on the circumstances surrounding us. And this joy comes in spite of our suffering, not because of it, as some who glorify suffering would have us believe.

These verses also tell us some significant things about trials. First, trials are often necessary, proving the genuineness of our faith and teaching us humility. Second, they are distressing, teaching us compassion so that we never make light of another's test or cruelly force them to smile while enduring it. And third, they come in various[1] forms.

This variety of trials is like different temperature settings on God's furnace. The settings are adjusted to burn off our dross, temper us, or soften us, according to what meets our highest need. It is in God's refining fires that the authenticity of our faith is revealed. The purpose of these fiery ordeals is that we may come forth as purified gold, a shining likeness of the Lord Jesus Himself (see Rom. 8:28–29). That glinting likeness is what ultimately gives glory and praise and honor to Christ.

---

1. The word comes from the Greek term *poikilos*, which means "variegated" or "many colored." The word is used in the New Testament for *various* diseases, *various* lusts, *various* miracles, and *various* strange doctrines. The one other time Peter uses this word is in 4:10 to describe the "manifold grace of God." There is no trial that God's grace can't match. It is sufficient, no matter how severe the suffering (2 Cor. 12:9).

We Have an Unseen Savior

And though you have not seen Him, you love Him, and though you do not see Him now, but believe in Him, you greatly rejoice with joy inexpressible and full of glory. (v. 8)

The context of this verse is suffering, remember? So we know that Peter's not giving us an inconsequential, theological hors d'oeuvre. He's giving us something we can sink our teeth into. He's telling us that our Savior is standing with us in that furnace even though we can't see Him.

Some, like the disciple Thomas, need to see and touch Jesus in order to believe. The Savior's words to the doubting disciple are instructive: "Blessed are they who did not see, and yet believed" (John 20:29). Even though we can't see Jesus beside us in our trials, He is there (see Ps. 23:4; Matt. 28:20; Heb. 13:5b)—just as He was when Shadrach, Meshach, and Abednego were thrown into the fiery furnace (Dan. 3:19–27).

We Have a Guaranteed Deliverance

Obtaining as the outcome of your faith the salvation of your souls. (v. 9)

The final passage of our faith is the deliverance of our souls, which includes not only a deliverance from present sin but a glorification of our physical bodies.

With the mention of this salvation or deliverance, Peter takes us on a literary interlude in which he suddenly addresses some questions that may have been under discussion in Christian circles in that day: What about earlier times in the days of the prophets? Did they grasp the full significance of this salvation? If not, how much did they comprehend?

Regarding Salvation: Why Prophets Were Curious

Those questions are answered, parenthetically, in verses 10–12.

As to this salvation, the prophets who prophesied of the grace that would come to you made careful search and inquiry, seeking to know what person or time the Spirit of Christ within them was indicating as He predicted the sufferings of Christ and the glories to follow. It was revealed to them that they were not serving themselves, but you, in these things which now have been announced to you through those who preached the gospel to you by the Holy Spirit sent from heaven—things into which angels long to look.

We're told here that the prophets wrote of the sufferings of Christ and of the glory that would ultimately be His. But verse 10 concludes that those prophets "made careful search and inquiry." Why? Because they didn't have access to two critical privileges that we have today.

First: *They didn't have a clear picture of God's full plan.* Looking ahead, they saw two mountain peaks—Mount Calvary and Mount Olivet. On one Christ would die in disgrace; on the other He would return in glory. What they couldn't see from their vantage point was that between these two mountains stretched a valley. This valley represented the church age, an era when God would extend His grace to the Gentiles.

Second: *They didn't have the Holy Spirit living within them as we do today.* The Spirit of God spoke to the prophets, spoke through them, inspired them, and ignited their message like a fire from heaven. But the benefits of the permanent indwelling of the Spirit were a total mystery to them. Like a blind lamplighter faithfully making his rounds on the streets of seventeenth-century London, the prophet lit lamps for the benefit of others, not himself.

A Personal Word

In concluding our lesson for today, we would like to address two categories of people who may read this material: those who suffer and those who seek.

To those who suffer: Only Christ's perspective can replace your resentment with rejoicing. Jesus is the central piece of suffering's puzzle. If you fit Him into place, the rest of the puzzle—no matter how dark and enigmatic—begins to make sense. That's when the rejoicing first begins to replace resentment.

To those who seek: Only Christ's salvation can change you from a spectator to a participant. You don't have to sit in the audience, watching. You can step out of your seat and onto the stage. You can play a part in the unfolding drama of redemption. The scenes will be demanding; some, even tragic. But then you will be able to understand the role that suffering plays in your life. And only then will you be able to smile through your suffering.

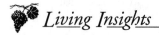 *Living Insights* _____ STUDY ONE

Romans 8:28–29a states that God's purpose for us is to make us into a great work of art—to conform us to the image of His Son.

> And we know that God causes all things to work together for good to those who love God, to those who are called according to His purpose. For whom He foreknew, He also predestined to become conformed to the image of His Son.

In his thought-provoking book *The Problem of Pain*, C. S. Lewis commented on the ramifications of this lofty creative vision that God has for our lives.

> We are, not metaphorically but in very truth, a Divine work of art, something that God is making, and therefore something with which He will not be satisfied until it has a certain character. Here again we come up against what I have called the "intolerable compliment." Over a sketch made idly to amuse a child, an artist may not take much trouble: he may be content to let it go even though it is not exactly as he meant it to be. But over the great picture of his life—the work which he loves, though in a different fashion, as intensely as a man loves a woman or a mother a child—he will take endless trouble— and would, doubtless, thereby *give* endless trouble to the picture if it were sentient. One can imagine a sentient picture, after being rubbed and scraped and re-commenced for the tenth time, wishing that it were only a thumb-nail sketch whose making was over in a minute. In the same way, it is natural for us to wish that God had designed for us a less glorious and less arduous destiny; but then we are wishing not for more love but for less.[2]

2. C. S. Lewis, *The Problem of Pain* (New York, N.Y.: Macmillan Co., 1962), pp. 42–43.

Thursday	**February 29**	Crucifixion, Proclamation, Resurrection, Exaltation
Friday	**March 1**	How to Shock the Pagan Crowd 1 Peter 4:1–6

Monday	**March 4**	How to Shock the Pagan Crowd
Tuesday	**March 5**	Four Commands . . . One Goal 1 Peter 4:7–11
Wednesday	**March 6**	Four Commands . . . One Goal
Thursday	**March 7**	When through Fiery Trials . . . 1 Peter 4:12–19
Friday	**March 8**	When through Fiery Trials . . .

Monday	**March 11**	Job Description for Shepherds 1 Peter 5:1–4
Tuesday	**March 12**	Job Description for Shepherds
Wednesday	**March 13**	A Formula That Brings Relief 1 Peter 5:5–7
Thursday	**March 14**	A Formula That Brings Relief
Friday	**March 15**	Standing Nose-to-Nose with the Adversary 1 Peter 5:8–11

Monday	**March 18**	Standing Nose-to-Nose with the Adversary
Tuesday	**March 19**	Reflections Seen in Peter's Ink 1 Peter 1–5
Wednesday	**March 20**	Reflections Seen in Peter's Ink
Thursday	**March 21**	Unraveling the Mystery of Suffering 2 Corinthians 1:1–11
Friday	**March 22**	Unraveling the Mystery of Suffering

Insight for Living • Post Office Box 69000, Anaheim, CA 92817-0900
Insight for Living Ministries • Post Office Box 2510, Vancouver, BC, Canada V6B 3W7
Insight for Living, Inc. • GPO Box 2823 EE, Melbourne, VIC 3001, Australia

Printed in the United States of America

Broadcast Schedule

Hope in Hurtful Times
A Study of 1 Peter

February 2–March 22, 1996

Friday	**February 2**	**Peter: The Man and His Message** Survey of 1 Peter
Monday	**February 5**	**Peter: The Man and His Message**
Tuesday	**February 6**	**How We Can Smile through Suffering** 1 Peter 1:1–12
Wednesday	**February 7**	**How We Can Smile through Suffering**
Thursday	**February 8**	**Staying Clean in a Corrupt Society** 1 Peter 1:13–21
Friday	**February 9**	**Staying Clean in a Corrupt Society**
Monday	**February 12**	**Reasons for Pulling Together** 1 Peter 1:22–2:3
Tuesday	**February 13**	**Reasons for Pulling Together**
Wednesday	**February 14**	**Several Portraits of Solid Saints** 1 Peter 2:4–12
Thursday	**February 15**	**Several Portraits of Solid Saints**
Friday	**February 16**	**Pressing On Even Though Ripped Off** 1 Peter 2:13–25
Monday	**February 19**	**Pressing On Even Though Ripped Off**
Tuesday	**February 20**	**The Give-and-Take of Domestic Harmony** 1 Peter 3:1–7
Wednesday	**February 21**	**The Give-and-Take of Domestic Harmony**
Thursday	**February 22**	**Maturity Checkpoints** 1 Peter 3:8–12
Friday	**February 23**	**Maturity Checkpoints**
Monday	**February 26**	**When Life "Just Ain't Fair"** 1 Peter 3:13–17
Tuesday	**February 27**	**When Life "Just Ain't Fair"**
Wednesday	**February 28**	**Crucifixion, Proclamation, Resurrection, Exaltation** 1 Peter 3:18–22

The rubbing and scraping on the dried canvas of our lives can be painful. But like da Vinci's Mona Lisa, the finished product will be well worth the waiting—and the suffering.

If the canvas of your life is resisting God's brush and turning out to be the "Moaning Lisa" instead, here are a few verses you may want to look up to give that painting the perspective it needs.

Proverbs 3:5	Romans 5:3–4
Isaiah 45:9	Romans 11:33–36
Isaiah 55:8–9	James 1:2–4
Isaiah 64:8	James 5:10–11

Remember, *only Christ's perspective can replace your resentment with rejoicing.*

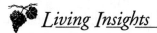 *Living Insights*

Once you become a Christian, the storms surrounding your life may not suddenly subside. In fact, they may even intensify. The difference is, you have the Master of the wind and the waves sitting beside you now in your boat, manning the helm and keeping you on an even keel.

Did becoming a Christian simplify your life or complicate it?

_____

_____

Are you presently going through some suffering? Describe it.

_____

_____

_____

_____

_____

In Philippians 3:10 Paul talks about the "fellowship of His sufferings." What do you think he means by that?

_____

_____

_____

Has your suffering led to a deeper fellowship with Christ? How?

_____

_____

_____

_____

_____

_____

Paul shares his perspective on suffering in Philippians 3:8–10. How does your perspective compare with his?

_____

_____

_____

_____

_____

_____

Chapter 3

STAYING CLEAN
IN A CORRUPT SOCIETY

1 Peter 1:13–21

Ⓗow can you stay clean in a corrupt society?

Some have suggested sanctification by isolation—withdrawing from the world as the only way to keep it from rubbing off on you. After all, how can you walk through a coal mine without getting dirty? The logic seems irrefutable. But the Bible offers a different tactic.

> Prove yourselves to be blameless and innocent, chil-
> dren of God above reproach in the midst of a
> crooked and perverse generation, among whom you
> appear as lights in the world. (Phil. 2:15)

Notice the words "in the midst of a crooked and perverse generation." Though we are not to be of the world, we are to be in the world. Shortly before He was arrested, Jesus prayed for His disciples about their relationship with the world. Mark His words carefully.

> "I have given them Thy word; and the world has
> hated them, because they are not of the world, even
> as I am not of the world. I do not ask Thee to take
> them out of the world, but to keep them from the
> evil one." (John 17:14–15)

Jesus doesn't ask the Father to isolate His disciples from the world but to *insulate* them, "to keep them from the evil one." In today's lesson we want to give a brief analysis of the world, make a strong challenge to be different from the world, and offer a few techniques to help us all stay clean in the corrupt world in which we live.

A Brief Analysis of Our World

When we use the term *world*, we're not thinking so much of a planet as we are a philosophy. The word is a figure of speech that encapsulates the mind-set and morality of the unregenerate. John talks of this philosophy in 1 John 2:15–17.

> Do not love the world, nor the things in the world. If anyone loves the world, the love of the Father is not in him. For all that is in the world, the lust of the flesh and the lust of the eyes and the boastful pride of life, is not from the Father, but is from the world. And the world is passing away, and also its lusts; but the one who does the will of God abides forever.

This world system is manipulated by the pervasive hand of Satan, who pulls the strings to achieve his wicked ends (5:19). If we are ever to extricate ourselves from those strings, we must first be able to see them and understand where they lead.

Its Philosophy

The world is designed to attract us with its sequined garb of fame, fortune, power, and pleasure. It winks an eye to gain our interest, flutters an eyelash to win our favor, and titillates us to get our support. Grammarian Kenneth Wuest comments:

> *Kosmos* refers to an ordered system. Here it is the ordered system of which Satan is the head, his fallen angels and demons are his emissaries, and the unsaved of the human race are his subjects. . . . Much in this world-system is religious, cultured, refined, and intellectual. But it is anti-God and anti-Christ.
> . . . This world of unsaved humanity is inspired by "the spirit of the age," . . . which Trench defines as follows: "All that floating mass of thoughts, opinions, maxims, speculations, hopes, impulses, aims, aspirations, at any time current in the world, which it may be impossible to seize and accurately define, but which constitutes a most real and effective power, being the moral, or immoral atmosphere which at every moment of our lives we inhale, again inevitably to exhale." This is the world-system to which John refers.[1]

---

1. Kenneth S. Wuest, *In These Last Days*, vol. 4, in *Wuest's Word Studies from the Greek New Testament* (Grand Rapids, Mich.: William B. Eerdmans Publishing Co., 1966), pp. 125–26.

Its Motivation

The world motivates us by appealing to our pride and the things that please us. Commentator M. R. Vincent defines it as "the sum-total of human life in the ordered world, considered apart from, alienated from, and hostile to God, and of the earthly things which seduce from God."[2]

Over all this realm, don't forget, Satan is prince. This provides us with the perfect background for our study in 1 Peter 1:13–21.

A Strong Challenge to Be Different

The pull of the world is every bit as strong and subtle as gravity. So invisible, yet so irresistible. So relentlessly there. Never absent or passive.

Living Our Lives in Holiness

Unless we realize how strong and how subtle the world's influence really is, we won't understand the passion behind Peter's words.

> Therefore, gird your minds for action, keep sober in spirit, fix your hope completely on the grace to be brought to you at the revelation of Jesus Christ. As obedient children, do not be conformed to the former lusts which were yours in your ignorance, but like the Holy One who called you, be holy yourselves also in all your behavior; because it is written, "You shall be holy, for I am holy." (1 Pet. 1:13–16)

Reading those four verses, you can't help but catch something of Peter's assertive spirit. He seems to be saying that this is no time to kick back; it isn't a day for passivity. Notice how strong his verbs are: "gird your minds . . . keep sober in spirit . . . fix your hope." It's easy to lose sight of that hope; easy to let the world intoxicate us and fuzz our minds. But if we're to shake ourselves out of that dizzying spell, we must resist the power it exerts on us (see Rom. 12:1–2).

Just as children inherit the nature of their parents, so we, as children of God, have inherited His nature. Furthermore, He's

---

2. M. R. Vincent, *Word Studies in the New Testament* (Wilmington, Del.: Associated Publishers and Authors, 1972), p. 389.

called us to follow in His footsteps—to be holy (1 Pet. 1:15–16). The term literally means "to be set apart" in some special and exclusive way. In holy matrimony, for example, a man and a woman are set apart, leaving all others as they cleave exclusively to each other. In holy communion, the bread and wine are set apart from common use and set aside to God alone. The same meaning lies behind the word *sanctify* in 1 Peter 3:15. We are to "sanctify" Christ as Lord in our hearts, or "set Him apart" as Lord. That's what 1 Peter 1:15–16 is aiming at.

Conducting Our Walk in Fear

Having God as our Father not only affects our nature but should also affect our attitude, as Peter states in verse 17.

> And if you address as Father the One who impartially judges according to each man's work, conduct yourselves in fear during the time of your stay upon earth.

Perhaps the term *reverence* should be preferred to "fear." The point is, if we're going to address God as Father, then we should conduct ourselves on earth in such a way that reflects our reverence for Him as our Father.

Almost parenthetically, Peter mentions the fact that God is the one who impartially judges our work. He alludes here to our appearing before Him at the judgment where we will all give an account of our lives (see Rom. 14:12; 2 Cor. 5:10). The details of that judgment are spelled out in 1 Corinthians 3:11–15.

Although we can't lose our salvation at that judgment, we can lose our reward. And that's something we all should fear. The loss of reward would be tantamount to an Olympian losing a gold medal because drug testing revealed the athlete's use of steroids.

But with the pride and pleasures of the *kosmos* so alluring, how can weaklings like us run the race without being disqualified and forfeiting our reward?

The solution to that problem has to do with our minds.

Focusing Our Minds on Christ

When the world pulls back its bowstring, our minds are the target. What arrows we allow to become impaled in our minds will ultimately poison our thoughts. And if we tolerate this long enough, we'll end up acting out what we think.

Verses 18–21 give us something to counteract that poison.

Verses 18–20 tell us what He has *done* for us. Verse 21 tells us what He has *given* us.

> Knowing that you were not redeemed with perishable things like silver or gold from your futile way of life inherited from your forefathers, but with precious blood, as of a lamb unblemished and spotless, the blood of Christ. For He was foreknown before the foundation of the world, but has appeared in these last times for the sake of you who through Him are believers in God, who raised Him from the dead and gave Him glory, so that your faith and hope are in God.

The first thing Christ did for us was to deliver us from slavery—slavery to a "futile way of life" (v. 18). Whether we knew it or not, we were trapped in a lifestyle that had only empty pleasures and dead-end desires to offer us. The only way for us to be emancipated from that slavery was to have someone redeem us, to pay the ransom price. That price was paid by Christ—not with gold or silver but with His precious blood (vv. 18–19).

The second thing Christ did for us was come near and make Himself known; He "appeared in these last times" (v. 20). Also in verse 20 underscore the words "for the sake of you." That makes the whole thing personal, doesn't it? He realized the enormity of our emptiness. He knew our inability to free ourselves. And He willingly stepped out of His privileged position in heaven to pay the ransom . . . for us (see also Phil. 2:5–8).

And what is it He gave? He gave Himself, a gift that not only allowed us to become free but to become secure, with our faith and hope resting not on our own shoulders, but on His (1 Pet. 1:21).

A Few Techniques to Remember

When we're in the comfortable conclave of Christian fellowship, it's easy to be holy, to conduct our lives in the fear of God, and to focus our minds on the Savior. But when we're in the world, when we're in a minority, it's different, isn't it?

If you want to stay clean, even when you're walking alone in the dark, low-ceilinged coal mine of the world, you need to remember a few things—four, to be specific.

First, *pay closer attention to what you look at* (v. 13; Col. 3:1–2).

Second, *give greater thought to the consequences of sin rather than its pleasures* (1 Pet. 1:14; Prov. 7). Third, *start each day by renewing your sense of reverence for God* (1 Pet. 1:17; 2 Cor. 7:1). Fourth, *periodically during each day focus fully on Christ* (1 Pet. 1:18–21; Heb. 12:2). Then you can experience what it's like to be in the world but not *of* it. Then you can walk through that coal mine—no matter how crooked and perverse it is—and stay clean.

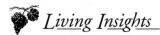 *Living Insights*

First John 2:15–16 warns against developing an inordinate affection for the world. In these verses we see the three avenues through which temptation comes to us. The first is through "the lust of the flesh." This would be an inordinate desire for anything that appeals to our body, from food to sex. Not that these are wrong when appreciated in perspective and satisfied in the proper context. But they shouldn't be the driving passion of our lives.

The second avenue of temptation is "the lust of the eyes," which refers to the compulsive drive to surround ourselves with things that appeal to the eye—beautiful things, ranging anywhere from fine china to designer clothes to scintillating jewelry. Is it wrong to possess these things? Certainly not. But it is wrong to have them possess us, to have their acquisition be the driving interest of our lives.

The third avenue is "the boastful pride of life"—the desire to be exalted and, in some way or another, worshiped. It can be the motivation of a movie star or a monk in the monastery. The position isn't important; it's what motivates the person to seek that position. With these three avenues of temptation in mind, turn to the temptation of Christ in Luke 4:1–13.

Which temptations correspond to those mentioned by John?

The lust of the flesh _____

The lust of the eyes _____

The boastful pride of life _____

What do you learn about the strategy of Satan from this account?

_____

_____

What do you learn about the strategy of Jesus?

_____

_____

_____

How did Jesus triumph over the devil during temptation (see James 4:7)?

_____

What temptation is presently trying to entice you away from an unswerving loyalty to the Lord?

_____

What things are you doing to resist it?

_____

_____

_____

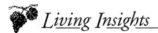 *Li̲ving Insights*_____ STUDY TWO

In the foreword to John White's insightful book *Flirting with the World*, Howard Snyder writes:

> Worldliness is the greatest threat to the church today. In other ages the church has suffered from dead orthodoxy, live heresy, flight from the world, and other maladies. But the painful truth today is that the church is guilty of massive accommodation to the world.[3]

3. Howard A. Snyder, "Forward" in *Flirting with the World*, rev. ed., by John White (Wheaton, Ill.: Harold Shaw Publishers, 1990), p. ix.

Look up the following verses on the Christian's relationship to the world. With each one, write down what the Spirit impresses on your heart in the way of observations, principles, or applications.

Matthew 6:24 _____

_____

_____

Matthew 6:25–34 _____

_____

_____

James 1:27 _____

_____

_____

Titus 2:11–14 _____

_____

_____

2 Peter 1:4 _____

_____

_____

Ephesians 2:1–7 _____

_____

_____

For further study on this subject, read John White's book *Flirting with the World*.

Chapter 4

REASONS FOR PULLING TOGETHER
1 Peter 1:22–2:3

Before Andrew Jackson became the seventh president of the United States, he served as a major general of the Tennessee militia. During the War of 1812 his troops reached an all-time low in their morale; a critical spirit grew up among them. They argued, bickered, and fought among themselves. It is reported that Jackson called them all together on one occasion when tensions were at their worst and said: "Gentlemen! Let's remember, the enemy is over *there!*"

His sobering reminder would be an appropriate word for the church today, wouldn't it?

The mark of the Christian should be unity and the love we have for one another (John 17:23; 13:35). But the mark of the church today bears neither of those two qualities. To our shame, we are looked on by the world as self-seeking and factious, not loving and unified. Stop in a Christian bookstore sometime and scan the shelves. What impression do you get? Do the books reflect love and unity within the body of Christ? Or do they reflect polarization, criticism, and judgment of one another? Better yet, sit back and observe what's going on in your own church. Are you overwhelmed with the love and unity that exudes from the body of believers? Or with the political power plays and petty problems that people have in getting along with one another?

Unity: An Almost Forgotten Virtue

To underscore this important quality, let's first turn our attention to the Upper Room Discourse in the Gospel of John, then to the teaching of Paul.

According to Jesus

All throughout His ministry Jesus taught and modeled the importance of unity. But His teaching and His example were never more compelling than the night of the Last Supper. There in the Upper Room He assumed the role of a servant and washed His

.sciples' feet. When He finished, Jesus said something unexpected.

> "Do you know what I have done to you? You call
> Me Teacher and Lord; and you are right, for so I am.
> If I then, the Lord and the Teacher, washed your
> feet, you also ought to wash one another's feet. For
> I gave you an example that you also should do as I
> did to you." (John 13:12–15)

Undoubtedly, the disciples expected Jesus to ask them to return the favor and wash His feet. Instead, He told them "to wash one another's feet." But in verses 34–35, the subject shifts from washing feet to showing love.

> "A new commandment I give to you, that you love
> one another, even as I have loved you, that you also
> love one another. By this all men will know that you
> are My disciples, if you have love for one another."

It's easy to love Christ, for all He is, for all He's done. It's not so easy, however, to love other Christians. Yet that is the command, and that compelling mark of the Christian will be a powerful witness to non-Christians.

Later on, as the oil lamps flickered away the night, Jesus prayed to the Father on behalf of His disciples (17:9–11), and for us as well (v. 20). And what did He pray for? Unity. Not uniformity, mind you, but unity; oneness, not sameness.

> "That they may all be one; even as Thou, Father,
> art in Me, and I in Thee, that they also may be in
> Us; that the world may believe that Thou didst send
> Me. And the glory which Thou hast given Me I
> have given to them; that they may be one, just as
> We are one; I in them, and Thou in Me, that they
> may be perfected in unity, that the world may know
> that Thou didst send Me, and didst love them, even
> as Thou didst love Me." (vv. 21–23)

According to Paul

The theme of unity is embroidered like a prominent motif throughout the fabric of Paul's teaching also. One such passage is found in Philippians 2:3–4.

> Do nothing from selfishness or empty conceit, but

with humility of mind let each of you regard one another as more important than himself; do not merely look out for your own personal interests, but also for the interests of others.

Sounds like something a teacher would say to a roomful of kindergartners, doesn't it? "Share. Don't be selfish. Think of others first." Yet how many adult problems could be solved if those two verses were the driving force in our relationship with one another? How many couples could resolve their differences? How many committees could resolve their disputes?

Love: A Never-to-Be-Forgotten Command

With the teachings of Christ and Paul as a backdrop, we'll be better able to understand and appreciate Peter's comments toward the end of his first chapter. As you turn there, remember, these Christians were hurting. They were scattered and living in extreme situations (1:1). They were going through various trials (1:6). And some, no doubt, were tempted to conform, compromise, or give up altogether (1:14–15).

Above all, these people needed to pull together. They needed the support of one another. They needed a community where they could find love and unity.

What Makes It Possible?

2/15/96

What frees us up so that we can be supportive of each other? The first half of verse 22 in 1 Peter 1 tells us.

Since you have in obedience to the truth purified your souls for a sincere love of the brethren . . .

Three things pop out of that passage: an obedience to the truth, a purity of soul, and a lack of hypocrisy.

Being obedient to the truth means that you don't look at others through the distorted lenses of your own biases. You see them as God sees them and love them as He loves them. This obedience to the truth has a purifying effect on us. It purges us not only of a limited perspective, but of prejudice, resentment, hurt feelings, and grudges. This purity of soul helps us love each other unhypocritically, with a sincere love. It doesn't make us blind to each other's faults; it merely gives us the grace to overlook them.

31

What Keeps It Strong?

Verse 22 finishes with the words,

Fervently love one another from the heart.

There is a passion here, a strong emotional commitment that is difficult to pick up on in the English. Two Greek words are predominantly used in the New Testament to describe love. One is *philos*, which generally refers to a brotherly love or the love of a friend. The other is *agapē*, a higher form of love, a more divine type of love (see 1 Cor. 13:4–7).

Although the root word in verse 22 is *philos*, it is intensified by Peter with the modifiers "fervently" and "from the heart."

Kenneth Wuest comments on what Peter means here.

> These Christians to whom Peter was writing already had a fondness and an affection for one another. The feeling of fondness and affection was perfectly proper in itself, but it could degenerate into an attachment for another which would be very selfish. But if these Christians would blend the two kinds of love, saturate the human fondness and affection with the divine love with which they are exhorted to love one another, then that human affection would be transformed and elevated to a heavenly thing. Then the fellowship of saint with saint would be a heavenly fellowship, glorifying to the Lord Jesus, and most blessed in its results to themselves. There is plenty of the *phile* fondness and affection among the saints, and too little of the *agapē* divine love.[1]

What are some reasons for pulling together and demonstrating this type of love toward one another? Peter gives us four, beginning in verse 23.

Support: Four Much-Needed Reminders

If we would all hear, learn, and review these four reminders, we would have much less trouble with disunity within the body of Christ.

---

1. Kenneth S. Wuest, *First Peter: In the Greek New Testament* (Grand Rapids, Mich.: William B. Eerdmans Publishing Co., 1956), p. 48.

First: We Are Children of the Same Father

For you have been born again. (v. 23a)

Being born again places us into a new family—the family of God (see John 1:12–13). If we are His children, it logically follows that we are related to each other as brothers and sisters.

Second: We Take Our Instruction from the Same Source

Not of seed which is perishable but imperishable, that is, through the living and abiding word of God. For,

"All flesh is like grass,
And all its glory like the flower of grass.
The grass withers,
And the flower falls off,
But the word of the Lord abides forever."
And this is the word which was preached to you.
(vv. 23b–25)

The seed is the Word of God (see also Matt. 13:1–23). But for that seed to grow and produce fruit in our lives, it must be embraced and applied, as James tells us.

Therefore putting aside all filthiness and all that remains of wickedness, in humility receive the word implanted, which is able to save your souls. But prove yourselves doers of the word, and not merely hearers who delude themselves. For if anyone is a hearer of the word and not a doer, he is like a man who looks at his natural face in a mirror; for once he has looked at himself and gone away, he has immediately forgotten what kind of person he was. But one who looks intently at the perfect law, the law of liberty, and abides by it, not having become a forgetful hearer but an effectual doer, this man shall be blessed in what he does. (James 1:21–25)

Although we may all hear the same Sunday morning message, unless our ears are attentive and our hearts prepared, that seed will be picked up in Satan's beak and winged right out of our life.

you hurt the family but not if you do applied

33

Third: We Have Our Struggles in the Same Realm

Therefore, putting aside all malice and all guile and
hypocrisy and envy and all slander . . . (1 Pet. 2:1)

These specific sins are the most frequent barriers to mutual
support. Let's look at them a little more closely.

Malice: The Greek word is a general word for the wickedness that
characterizes unbelievers entrenched in the world system. These
sins would be categorized as those that would hurt and injure others.

Guile: The Greek word means two-facedness or trickery. The
earliest form of the word meant "to catch with bait." It refers to a
deception that is aimed at attaining one's own end. *Hidew*

Hypocrisy: The Greek word means to act a part, hide behind a
mask, or appear to be someone you're not.

Envy: Envy involves hidden resentment over another's advantage and wanting that advantage for yourself. Edward Gordon Selwyn comments on the Greek text, saying that this sin is "a constant
plague of all voluntary organizations, not least religious organizations, and to which even the Twelve themselves were subject at
the very crisis of our Lord's ministry."[2]

Slander: Literally, the word means "evil speaking." It occurs most
often when the victim is not there to offer a defense or set the
record straight. It is especially prevalent when a rumor is being
passed around regarding someone. Slander is disparaging gossip that
destroys our confidence in an individual and weakens that person's
reputation.

And what does Peter command us to do with these five outdated
garments that belong to our old nature? He tells us to put them
aside; literally to "strip them off" (v. 1).

Fourth: We Focus Our Attention on the Same Objective

Like newborn babes, long for the pure milk of the
word, that by it you may grow in respect to salvation,
if you have tasted the kindness of the Lord. (vv. 2–3)

What is the objective? Maturity. And our model? The Lord
Himself. For three and one-half years Peter followed Jesus everywhere
He went. Why? He had tasted "the kindness of the Lord." Suckled
on that kindness, Peter grew to maturity. And so can we!

---

2. Edward Gordon Selwyn, *The First Epistle of St. Peter,* 2d ed. (1947; reprint, London,
England: Macmillan Press, 1974), p. 153.

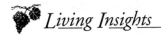 *Living Insights*

According to Philippians 2:1–8, selflessly giving ourselves to one another is the key to unity. Notice in the passage how the exhortations about our relationships with others are all built upon the example of the selflessness Christ first demonstrated.

> If therefore there is any encouragement in Christ, if there is any consolation of love, if there is any fellowship of the Spirit, if any affection and compassion, make my joy complete by being of the same mind, maintaining the same love, united in spirit, intent on one purpose. Do nothing from selfishness or empty conceit, but with humility of mind let each of you regard one another as more important than himself; do not merely look out for your own personal interests, but also for the interests of others. Have this attitude in yourselves which was also in Christ Jesus, who, although He existed in the form of God, did not regard equality with God a thing to be grasped, but emptied Himself, taking the form of a bond-servant, and being made in the likeness of men. And being found in appearance as a man, He humbled Himself by becoming obedient to the point of death, even death on a cross.

How many marriages could be mended if Philippians 2 were applied to the relationship? How many fractured friendships could be put back together? How many divided churches?

Make a photocopy of the passage quoted above, paste it on a three-by-five-inch card, and review it periodically until you've memorized it. Probably no other passage of Scripture is as helpful in making relationships work as this one is. So don't stop at memorizing it. Make it a part of your life.

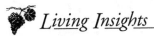 *Living Insights*

First Peter 2:1 tells us that if we're to go on to maturity, we have to discard some of the things hanging in the closet of our old nature. Another passage that talks about unity and growing up and laying aside the garments of our old nature is Ephesians 4. Take a few minutes to read over the chapter, then answer the following questions.

What are some other remnants of our old nature that we should lay aside?

_____   _____

_____   _____

_____   _____

What are some of the unifying clothes from our new nature that we should put on?

_____   _____

_____   _____

_____   _____

What is the blueprint we should follow when building up the body?

_____

What key phrase is used three times in verses 1–16?

_____

In verses 17–32? _____

Paul exhorts us in verse 32 to forgive each other "just as God in Christ also has forgiven you." Describe how God has forgiven you. For example: completely _____

_____

_____

Now focus on a fractured relationship you have with someone within the body of Christ. How would that relationship change if you forgave that person the way God has forgiven you?

_____

_____

_____

_____

Chapter 5

SEVERAL PORTRAITS
OF SOLID SAINTS

1 Peter 2:4–12

For some unexplainable reason, we have a tendency to outgrow a close friendship with God. When we were children, we felt free and open with our heavenly Father. But when we became adults, we seemed to take a few giant steps backward in our relationship with Him.

The ease with which we once approached God can be seen in the letters written to Him by children. See if the ones below don't take you back to a time of innocence and openness in your own relationship with Him.

> Dear Lord,
>   Thank you for the nice day today. You even fooled the T.V. weatherman.
>   Hank (age 7)

> Dear Lord,
>   Do you ever get mad.
>   My mother gets mad all the time but she is only a human.
>   Yours truly,
>   David (age 8)

> Dear Lord,
>   I need a raise in my allowance. Could you have one of your angels tell my father.
>   Thank you.
>   David (age 7)[1]

> Dear God,
>   Charles my cat got run over. And if you made it happen you have to tell me why.
>   Harvey

---

1. Quoted in *Dear Lord*, comp. Bill Adler (Nashville, Tenn.: Thomas Nelson Publishers, 1982), n.p.

Dear God,

Can you guess what is the biggest river of all of them? The Amazon.

You ought to be able to because you made it. Ha, ha.

Guess who.[2]

It would be interesting to compile an assortment of adult letters to God, wouldn't it? Undoubtedly, the childhood innocence would be lost, as well as the ease of approach. The words would be more guarded. Fear and feelings of worthlessness would underscore our halting sentences. Guilt and regret would punctuate our paragraphs. We have lost much, haven't we, on the road to adulthood? Although we can't turn back the clock, we can turn back our hearts. Let's do that now as we delve into 1 Peter 2, a passage where God gives His appraisal of us as His children.

Let's Be Reminded of God's Appraisal of Us

In the Old Testament, God reveals some encouraging things about our relationship with Him: His plans are for our welfare (Jer. 29:11); He shows us lovingkindness and has compassion on us as a father has on his own children (Ps. 103:1–5, 11–14); and He is good to us (Lam. 3:25).

In the New Testament, God continues to reveal His paternal care for us: He has redeemed us, given us an inheritance, and shown us forgiveness (Col. 1:12–14); and He has given us good gifts from heaven (James 1:17). The most succinct summary of God's appraisal of our relationship as His children can be found in Romans 8:31–32.

> What then shall we say to these things? If God is for us, who is against us? He who did not spare His own Son, but delivered Him up for us all, how will He not also with Him freely give us all things?

Contrary to popular opinion, God doesn't sit in heaven with His jaws clenched and His arms folded in disapproval. He is not ticked off at His children for all the times they trip over their tiny feet and fall flat on their diapers. He is a loving Father, and we are precious in His sight, the delight of His life.

---

2. Quoted in *More Children's Letters to God,* comp. Eric Marshall and Stuart Hample (New York, N.Y.: Simon and Schuster, Essandess Special Editions, 1967), n.p.

Turning to 1 Peter, we catch a glimpse of this delight in the way God refers to us.

Some Specific Titles God Gives Us

In 1 Peter 2:4–10, six titles stand out that reflect God's affirming evaluation of us. *2/19/96*

We Are Living Stones in a Spiritual House

> And coming to Him as to a living stone, rejected by men, but choice and precious in the sight of God, you also, as living stones, are being built up as a spiritual house for a holy priesthood, to offer up spiritual sacrifices acceptable to God through Jesus Christ. For this is contained in Scripture:
>
> "Behold I lay in Zion a choice stone, a precious corner stone,
> And he who believes in Him shall not be disappointed."
> This precious value, then, is for you who believe. But for those who disbelieve,
> "The stone which the builders rejected,
> This became the very corner stone,"
> and,
> "A stone of stumbling and a rock of offense";
> for they stumble because they are disobedient to the word, and to this doom they were also appointed. (vv. 4–8)

The metaphor that's extended through this passage is that of a building, Christ being the cornerstone and we being the living stones that make up the building.[3]

Each time someone trusts Christ as Savior, another stone is quarried out of the pit of sin and cemented into place through the work of the Holy Spirit. And carefully overseeing this construction is Christ, who is the hands-on contractor of this eternal edifice (see Matt. 16:18).[4]

---

3. Paul uses the same image in Ephesians 2:19–22.

4. In the old covenant, God dwelt among His people in a physical temple (1 Kings 9:3). In the new covenant, God does not dwell in a localized place but in the hearts of all His children (1 Cor. 3:16–17; 6:19).

All kinds of prophets of doom wonder about the condition of God's building. They see it more as condemned property, dilapidated and derelict, than as the edifice of a master plan that is being constructed on schedule. The truth is, God is the master architect, and every stone is being placed exactly where He designed it.

We Are Priests in the Same Temple

> You also, as living stones, are being built up as a spiritual house for a *holy priesthood*, to offer up spiritual sacrifices acceptable to God through Jesus Christ. . . . But you are a chosen race, a *royal priesthood*, a holy nation, a people for God's own possession, that you may proclaim the excellencies of Him who has called you out of darkness into His marvelous light. (1 Pet. 2:5, 9, emphasis added)

One verse refers to us as a "holy priesthood" while the other refers to us as a "royal priesthood." It's true that we're not all preachers or evangelists or teachers. But we're all priests, belonging to a kingly order that has been set apart by God.

The role of priest implies more than meets the eye, for priests have specific responsibilities delineated in Scripture. Priests offer up prayers, bring spiritual sacrifices, intercede to God on behalf of others, and stay in tune with the spiritual side of life. All this applies to every believer. Regardless of age. Regardless of sex. Regardless of social standing. *He 13 V15 - PRAise*

We Are a Chosen Race

> But you are a *chosen race*. (v. 9, emphasis added)

Our heads might have a tendency to swell at being chosen to be on God's team, so if you'll turn back to Deuteronomy 7:6–8, we'll put this whole idea of being chosen by God into perspective.

Here Moses is addressing the nation Israel, preparing them to enter the Promised Land.

> "For you are a holy people to the Lord your God; the Lord your God has chosen you to be a people for His own possession out of all the peoples who are on the face of the earth. The Lord did not set His love on you nor choose you because you were more in number than any of the peoples, for you

were the fewest of all peoples, but because the Lord loved you and kept the oath which He swore to your forefathers, the Lord brought you out by a mighty hand, and redeemed you from the house of slavery, from the hand of Pharaoh king of Egypt."

Why did God choose the Hebrews to be His people? Because of their strength? Because of their numbers? Because of their mental or moral superiority? No. He chose them simply because of His grace—a kindness shown to them entirely without merit on their part. By application, God's choice of us was not based on anything we did to impress Him. It wasn't the size of our faith . . . or the sincerity. It wasn't the goodness of our heart . . . or the greatness of our intellect. It wasn't even because we first chose Him. It was entirely by grace (see also John 15:16).

We Are a Holy Nation

Aside from being a chosen race, Peter tells us in verse 9 that we are a holy nation, set apart to God and for His special purposes. The apostle Paul also talks about this in his letter to the Philippians.

> For our citizenship is in heaven, from which also we eagerly wait for a Savior, the Lord Jesus Christ. (Phil. 3:20)

If we seem out of step with the world, it is because we march to the beat of a different drummer. We sing a different national anthem and pledge our allegiance to a different flag—because our citizenship, our true citizenship, is in heaven.

We Are a People for God's Own Possession

First Peter 2:9 also says we are "a people for God's own possession." The value of even the most common things is enhanced if owned by someone significant. A book that once sat on Lincoln's shelf. A desk where Churchill wrote his memoirs. A pipe owned by C. S. Lewis. Sheet music handwritten by Beethoven. A house once owned by Hemingway. Now think of the value of something owned by God. What incredible worth that bestows on us. What inexplicable dignity.

We Are God's People Who Have Received Mercy

For you once were not a people, but now you are

the people of God; you had not received mercy, but now you have received mercy. (v. 10)

As a result of God's mercy, we have become a people who are uniquely and exclusively owned by God. First Corinthians 6:19–20 says,

Or do you not know that your body is a temple of the Holy Spirit who is in you, whom you have from God, and that you are not your own? For you have been bought with a price: therefore glorify God in your body.

The fact that we are not our own makes all the difference in the world as to how we live. That's the whole point of Peter's applicational summary in verses 11–12.

A Few Responses to God from Us

Peter concludes his thought by telling us that, in light of all that we are as God's children, we are to live in a certain way.

Beloved, I urge you as aliens and strangers to abstain from fleshly lusts, which wage war against the soul. Keep your behavior excellent among the Gentiles, so that in the thing in which they slander you as evildoers, they may on account of your good deeds, as they observe them, glorify God in the day of visitation. (1 Pet. 2:11–12)

For unbelievers, earth is a playground where the flesh is free to romp and run wild. But for believers, earth is a battleground. It's the place where we combat the lusts that wage war against our souls. For the brief tour of duty we Christians have on this earth, Peter gives us four suggestions.

First: *Live a clean life.* Never assume that it makes no difference to unbelievers how Christians live. We live out our faith before a watching world. That's why Peter urges us to abstain from fleshly lusts, in order to get their attention and to prove that what we believe works.

Second: *Leave no room for slander.* When the ancient Greek philosopher Plato was told that a certain man had been making slanderous charges against him, his response was, "I will live in such a way that no one will believe what he says."[5] The most convincing

5. Plato, quoted by William Barclay in *The Letters of James and Peter*, rev. ed., The Daily Study Bible Series (Philadelphia, Pa.: Westminster Press, 1976), p. 203.

defense is the silent integrity of our character, not how vociferously we deny the charges.

Third: _Do good deeds among unbelievers._ Our good deeds should not be limited to the family of God, but should also extend to those outside the family (see Matt. 5:46–47; Luke 6:34–36). What makes the story of the Good Samaritan so compelling? The merciful deeds were done on behalf of a total stranger (Luke 10:30–37). That is how we win the right to be heard—not by a slick, mass-advertising campaign, but by our actions.

Fourth: _Never forget—you are being watched._ The world is watching us to see if what we believe is true, as this story told by Warren Wiersbe illustrates.

> In the summer of 1805, a number of Indian chiefs and warriors met in council at Buffalo Creek, New York, to hear a presentation of the Christian message by a Mr. Cram from the Boston Missionary Society. After the sermon, a response was given by Red Jacket, one of the leading chiefs. Among other things, the chief said: . . .
>
> "Brother, we are told that you have been preaching to the white people in this place. These people are our neighbors. We are acquainted with them. We will wait a little while and see what effect your preaching has upon them. If we find it does them good, makes them honest and less disposed to cheat Indians, we will then consider again of what you have said."[6]

🍇 _Living Insights_

Write out any of your own observations about the metaphors Peter used to describe the believer in 1 Peter 2:4–12, especially noting any applications to your life.

Living stones: _____

_____

6. Warren W. Wiersbe, _Be Hopeful_ (Wheaton, Ill.: SP Publications, Victor Books, 1982), p. 57.

Spiritual house: _____

_____

Holy priesthood: _____

_____

Chosen race: _____

_____

Royal priesthood: _____

_____

Holy nation: _____

_____

People for God's own possession: _____

_____

Aliens and strangers: _____

_____

🍇 *Living Insights* _____ STUDY TWO

To get an even stronger grasp of Peter's applicational summary
in verses 11–12, let's dig into some cross references that also
encourage us to live lives of distinction.

Galatians 5:16–26 contrasts the deeds of the flesh with the fruit
of the Spirit. Make as many observations as you can about each.

Deeds of the flesh: _____

_____

_____

_____

_____

Fruit of the Spirit: _____

_____

_____

_____

_____

Look up Matthew 5:13–16, and make as many observations as you can about the two metaphors used to describe the Christian's influence in the world.

Salt: _____

_____

_____

_____

_____

Light: _____

_____

_____

_____

_____

What do these two metaphors have in common?

_____

From Philippians 2:14–15, how is the light of our lives held high so as to stand out in stark contrast to those who live in darkness?

_____

_____

_____

2/20/96

Chapter 6

PRESSING ON
EVEN THOUGH RIPPED OFF
1 Peter 2:13–25

Ever bought a lemon of a used car? Ever dropped six dollars on a movie that made the home video of your family vacation look like *The Sound of Music?*

Who hasn't been hoodwinked by a smooth-talking salesman with styled hair and patent leather shoes? Who hasn't been burned by a glitzy Hollywood ad campaign that promises more than it delivers?

But rip-offs like those are relatively easy to recover from. What's more difficult to endure is when the suffering gets a little more personal—when someone slanders your reputation, pulls the economic rug out from under you, or threatens your life.

If you've ever been treated like that, you're in good company. David was ripped off by Saul; Esau, by Jacob; Joseph, by his brothers; Job, by the Sabeans and Chaldeans. But although misery may love company, company doesn't alleviate the pain of unfair treatment.

Natural Reactions to Unfair Treatment

When we're treated unfairly, three common, knee-jerk reactions seem to come naturally.

First: *There is the aggressive pattern: to place blame on others.* This reaction not only focuses on the person who ripped us off and keeps a running tally of wrongs done against us, but it also engineers ways to get back and get even. It starts seminally with a seed of resentment, germinates into revenge, and grows a deep root of bitterness that tenaciously wraps around our hearts.

Second: *There is the passive pattern: to feel sorry for ourselves.* We throw a pity party, whining and complaining to whomever will lend a sympathetic ear. But if we wallow in that slough of despond too long, we will become depressed and immobile. Like quicksand, feeling sorry for ourselves will suck us under.

Third: *There is the holding pattern: to postpone feelings.* This is the Scarlett O'Hara syndrome: "I'll think about it tomorrow." Every boiling issue is left to simmer by placing it on the back burner over

46

a low flame. On the surface all seems calm; but underneath, our feelings seethe. This failure to deal with the problem forthrightly leads only to doubt and disillusionment.

An Alternative That Honors God

2/23/06

Pressed between the pages of 1 Peter is a roselike reminder that fragrantly informs us how to press on even when we've been ripped off. But as you turn there, don't expect to find any of the three patterns we've just described. Expect instead an alternative reaction to unfair treatment.

The Command

> Submit yourselves for the Lord's sake to every human institution, whether to a king as the one in authority, or to governors as sent by him for the punishment of evildoers and the praise of those who do right. (1 Pet. 2:13–14)

It's important to understand the historical context of this command. The Roman Empire, throughout which the readers of 1 Peter were scattered, was not a benevolent monarchy. It was a dictatorship ruled by the insane demagogue Nero, who was notorious for his wickedness and his cruelty to Christians.

Here was the problem: Should the Christians pick up arms and resist a government with such a leader at its helm? Peter said no. Nowhere in Scripture is anarchy promoted. The believer was not put on earth to overthrow governments but to establish in the human heart a kingdom not of this world. This doesn't mean we buckle under by compromising our convictions or renouncing our faith. It does mean that we are to render unto Caesar the coin of civil obedience. It means we are not only to pray for those in authority (1 Tim. 2:1–2), but to live honorably under their domain (Rom. 13:1–3).

The way to live honorably, Peter says, is to "submit" (see also 1 Pet. 2:18; 3:1, 5). The Greek word is *hupotassō*. It's a military term that means "to fall in rank under an authority." It's composed of two words, *tassō*, meaning "to appoint, order, or arrange," and *hupo*, meaning "to place under or to subordinate." In this particular construction it conveys the idea of subjecting oneself or placing oneself under another.

This recognition of existing authority, coupled with a willingness

47

to set aside one's own personal desires, shows a deep dependence upon God (compare 2:23). This submission to authority is not only in respect to God, the foremost human authority, but to lesser officials as well—kings and governors.

The Reason

For such is the will of God that by doing right you
may silence the ignorance of foolish men. (v. 15)

The Greek word for silence means "to close the mouth with a muzzle" (see also 1 Cor. 9:9). Loose-jawed rumors about Christians gossiped their way through the Roman Empire—about their secret meetings; their subversive ideologies; their loyalty to another kingdom; their plans to infiltrate, indoctrinate, and lead an insurrection. To muzzle these rumors, Peter encouraged submission to the powers that be.[1]

The Principle

Act as free men, and do not use your freedom as a
covering for evil, but use it as bondslaves of God.
Honor all men; love the brotherhood, fear God,
honor the king. (1 Pet. 2:16–17)

These five commands come like an enfilade of gunfire, hitting the reader in rapid succession. The principle we want to consider comes out of the longer command in verse 16, which states that our freedom shouldn't be a covering for evil. The word covering paints a vivid picture of someone holding a cloak over something. We must be careful that the comfortable clothing of freedom is never stretched to conceal our own wickedness.

An Example and the Example

Next, Peter addresses slaves in particular.

Servants, be submissive to your masters with all
respect, not only to those who are good and gentle,
but also to those who are unreasonable. For this finds
favor, if for the sake of conscience toward God a
man bears up under sorrows when suffering unjustly.

---

1. These powers may have the right to establish codes and regulations, but they do not have the right to dictate what we can preach in our pulpits or teach in our Christian schools. When they cross that line, they transgress the boundary of their God-ordained authority (see Acts 4:5–20).

48

For what credit is there if, when you sin and are harshly treated, you endure it with patience? But if when you do what is right and suffer for it you patiently endure it, this finds favor with God. For you have been called for this purpose. (vv. 18–21a)

William Barclay sheds some historical light on slavery to illuminate the meaning of these verses.

> In the time of the early church . . . there were as many as 60,000,000 slaves in the Roman Empire. . . .
>
> It was by no means only menial tasks which were performed by slaves. Doctors, teachers, musicians, actors, secretaries, stewards were slaves. In fact, all the work of Rome was done by slaves. Roman attitude was that there was no point in being master of the world and doing one's own work. Let the slaves do that and let the citizens live in pampered idleness. The supply of slaves would never run out.
>
> Slaves were not allowed to marry; but they cohabited; and the children born of such a partnership were the property of the master, not of the parents, just as the lambs born to the sheep belonged to the owner of the flock, and not to the sheep.
>
> It would be wrong to think that the lot of slaves was always wretched and unhappy, and that they were always treated with cruelty. Many slaves were loved and trusted members of the family; but one great inescapable fact dominated the whole situation. In Roman law a slave was not a person but a thing; and he had absolutely no legal rights whatsoever. For that reason there could be no such thing as justice where a slave was concerned. . . . Peter Chrysologus sums the matter up: "Whatever a master does to a slave, undeservedly, in anger, willingly, unwillingly, in forgetfulness, after careful thought, knowingly, unknowingly, is judgment, justice and law." In regard to a slave, his master's will, and even his master's caprice, was the only law.[2]

2. William Barclay, *The Letters of James and Peter*, rev. ed., The Daily Study Bible Series (Philadelphia, Pa.: Westminster Press, 1976), pp. 210–11.

It would have been easy for slaves who became Christians to think that their Christianity gave them the freedom to break with their masters. But this was not so. Although Christianity gradually pervaded the culture and overcame slavery, it didn't do so in the first century. The Scriptures, therefore, weren't immediately concerned with changing the social order; they were concerned with the more ultimate priority—changing the human heart (compare 1 Cor. 7:20–24).

And the natural tendency of the human heart is to fight back against unfair and unreasonable treatment. But Peter's point is that seeking revenge for unjust suffering is a sign of self-appointed lordship over one's own affairs. Revenge, then, is totally inappropriate for one who has submitted to the lordship of Jesus Christ. Christians must stand in contrast to those around them. This includes a difference in attitude and a difference in focus. Our attitude should be "submissive"; our focus, "toward God" (1 Pet. 2:18). And how is this change in heart viewed by God? It "~~finds favor~~ grace" with Him (v. 19).

Our focus, then, should not be consumed with getting the raise at the office but getting the praise from God, not with getting the glory for ourselves but giving the glory to Him (see 1 Cor. 10:31; Col. 3:17).

When we lose sight of this fact, we begin to take the pressure personally, resenting our work as we embroider our revenge. To combat that reaction, we need to realize the truth of 1 Peter 2:21— that suffering unjustly is part and parcel of our calling. How do we know this? Because of the example set by the Savior Himself.

> Since Christ also suffered for you, leaving you an example for you to follow in His steps, who committed no sin, nor was any deceit found in His mouth; and while being reviled, He did not revile in return; while suffering, He uttered no threats, but kept entrusting Himself to Him who judges righteously; and He Himself bore our sins[3] in His body on the cross, that we might die to sin and live to

3. The phrase "bore our sins" in verse 24 contains the same term used in the Greek Old Testament for the priest carrying the sacrifice to the altar. The brazen altar was four and one-half feet high, and priests had to walk on an incline to reach it, "bearing" the sacrifice as they did so.

righteousness; for by His wounds[4] you were healed.
(vv. 21b–24)

In these verses Peter shifts from *an* example of unfair treatment to *the* example that we should follow, from that of a servant to that of the Savior.

Peter had seen firsthand the yoke of unjust suffering placed upon Jesus' shoulders. He saw the rejection of society and the retaliation of the Sanhedrin. He saw Jesus betrayed by a friend and brutalized by an empire. Peter himself denied Him. Yet in the Savior's innocent eyes was no windswept harbor of revenge. They were placid under the storm of unjust suffering. And they offered the cool drink of forgiveness for friend and foe alike.

Romans 6 (handwritten annotation)

A Benefit That Accompanies Such Obedience

Staring in horror at the Cross, one can't help but become dizzy from a swarm of questions. Why? Why should this innocent man endure such unjust suffering? Why should we? Why shouldn't we resist the thorns and retaliate against the nails of the cross we are forced to bear? Why should we submit to the cross of unjust suffering?

Because it causes us to return to our Shepherd for protection.

> For you were continually straying like sheep, but now you have returned to the Shepherd and Guardian of your souls. (v. 25)

Are you feeling the splinters of some cross of unjust suffering? Has a friend betrayed you? Has an employer impaled you? Has a disaster been dropped on your life that's almost too great to bear? If so, don't fight back; find your way back to the Good Shepherd who endured the cross and laid down His life . . . for you.

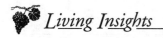 *Living Insights*

STUDY ONE

Submission is not a popular word today, yet the Bible seems to indicate that it is key to making relationships work. Look up the following passages, and write down the relationship each exhortation for submission applies to.

4. The word "wounds" in verse 24 is singular in Greek. It is a picture of one massive welt, oozing with blood. Such was His appearance on the cross (see Isa. 53:5).

51

Romans 13:1 _____

Ephesians 5:21 _____

Ephesians 6:1 _____

Timothy 2:11 _____

Hebrews 13:17 _____

James 4:7 _____

1 Peter 2:13 _____

1 Peter 2:18 _____

1 Peter 3:1 _____

1 Peter 5:5 _____

In which of these relationships is it most difficult for you to submit?

_____

Why do you think that is?

_____

_____

_____

_____

_____

_____

What is the character quality necessary to help us become more submissive (see James 4:6–7; 1 Pet. 5:5–6)?

_____

_____

🍇 *Living Insights* _____ STUDY TWO

If you're enduring suffering right now, especially unjust suffering, it can be a dizzying experience. To keep your balance in those times, when things are swirling around you, it's important to find a fixed point and focus on it. Lamentations 3:25–32 is just such a reference point.

> The Lord is good to those who wait for Him,
> To the person who seeks Him.
> It is good that he waits silently
> For the salvation of the Lord.
> It is good for a man that he should bear
> The yoke in his youth.
> Let him sit alone and be silent
> Since He has laid it on him.
> Let him put his mouth in the dust,
> Perhaps there is hope.
> Let him give his cheek to the smiter;
> Let him be filled with reproach.
> For the Lord will not reject forever,
> For if He causes grief,
> Then He will have compassion
> According to His abundant lovingkindness.

How does the advice in this passage help you in your present situation of suffering?

_____

_____

_____

_____

_____

After meditating on the passage and applying its principles to your own predicament, personalize the individual verses and use them as a prayer list.

Chapter 7

THE GIVE-AND-TAKE
OF DOMESTIC HARMONY
1 Peter 3:1–7

In his book *Secrets to Inner Beauty*, Joe Aldrich humorously describes the realities of married life.

> It doesn't take long for the newlyweds to discover that "everything in one person nobody's got." They soon learn that a marriage license is just a learner's permit, and ask with agony, "Is there life after marriage?"
>
> An old Arab proverb states that marriage begins with a prince kissing an angel and ends with a bald-headed man looking across the table at a fat lady. Socrates told his students, "By all means marry. If you get a good wife, twice blessed you will be. If you get a bad wife, you'll become a philosopher." Count Herman Keyserling said it well when he stated that "The essential difficulties of life do not end, but rather begin with marriage."[1]

Marriage starts out like a romantic, moonlit sleigh ride, smoothly gliding over the glistening snow. It's living together after the honeymoon that turns out to be rough sledding. For two people to live in domestic harmony, it takes a lot of give-and-take, and we'll learn how to do some of this as we study 1 Peter 3:1–7.

A Few Words of Review

Before we plunge into these seven significant verses, let's take a step back and review their context. The overall setting starts at 2:13 and continues through the end of chapter 3. This passage challenges us to respond correctly even in unfair circumstances. Some of those circumstances are briefly illustrated: citizens in various circumstances (2:13–17), slaves with unfair masters (vv. 18–20),

---

1. Joseph C. Aldrich, *Secrets to Inner Beauty* (Santa Ana, Calif.: Vision House Publishers, 1977), pp. 87–88.

54

Christ with unfair accusers (vv. 21–25), wives with unfair husbands (3:1–6), and Christians in an unfair society (vv. 13–17).

The key term in this section is the word *submit*. The Greek word, *hupotassō*, has military roots and means "to fall in rank under the authority of another . . . to subject oneself for the purpose of obeying or pleasing another."

Some have taken this word to the extreme, promoting obsequious behavior by women in the face of the worst kinds of abuse. Others have taken the other extreme and labeled these passages culturally obsolete, with application only to the era in which they were originally written. The balance of the biblical position lies somewhere in between these two poles.

Wise Counsel to Wives

The first six verses of our passage refer to wives.[2] Into the fabric of these verses are woven no less than four implied imperatives.

Analyze Your Actions

> In the same way, you wives, be submissive to your own husbands so that even if any of them are disobedient to the word, they may be won without a word by the behavior of their wives, as they observe your chaste and respectful behavior. (1 Pet. 3:1–2)

The tendency of many wives is to view their role in a conditional way that depends on the behavior of their husbands: "I'll be the kind of wife I should be if he's the kind of husband *he* should be." This passage, however, doesn't let the woman off the hook that easily. Peter has specifically included "disobedient" husbands in verse 1, so he clearly has in mind women whose husbands aren't measuring up to God's standard.

Having to exhibit godly behavior when their husbands aren't, however, sometimes produces another tendency—substituting secret

---

2. "It may seem strange that Peter's advice to wives is six times as long as that to husbands. This is because the wife's position was far more difficult than that of the husband. If a husband became a Christian, he would automatically bring his wife with him into the Church and there would be no problem. But if a wife became a Christian while her husband did not, she was taking a step which was unprecedented and which produced the acutest problems." William Barclay, *The Letters of James and Peter*, rev. ed., The Daily Study Bible Series (Philadelphia, Pa.: Westminster Press, 1976), p. 218.

manipulation for a quiet spirit. This manipulation may take many forms: pouting, sulking, scheming, bargaining, nagging, preaching, coercing, humiliating. But wives who use this strategy are not trusting God to change their husbands' lives. They're trusting in themselves.

Peter is saying something to these wives: "You are responsible for *you*—not for your husband. That's God's job." And wives who are truly obedient to Christ will find that He will honor their secure spirit. Yes, submission is a mark of security. It is not a spineless cringing, based on insecurity and fear. It is a voluntary unselfishness, a willing and cooperative spirit that seeks the highest good of her husband (compare Prov. 31:10–12). As he observes[3] her compelling behavior—the silent eloquence of a lovely life—his heart will eventually soften toward spiritual things.

Watch Your Adornment

> And let not your adornment be merely external—
> braiding the hair, and wearing gold jewelry, or put-
> ting on dresses. (1 Pet. 3:3)

The outer adornment in verse 3 forms a contrast with the inner adornment we'll see in verse 4. It's easy, particularly in our shop-till-you-drop culture, to let externals get out of balance. The point of the contrast is to restore that balance.

What clues us into the need for balance is the word *merely*. It was added by the editors of the New American Standard Bible to help the reader understand Peter's intended meaning. Peter isn't prohibiting the braiding of hair or the wearing of jewelry any more than he's prohibiting the putting on of dresses. He merely wants to put those things in the background and bring the woman's character into the foreground. Perspective is the key.

Check Your Attitude

> But let it be the hidden person of the heart, with
> the imperishable quality of a gentle and quiet spirit,
> which is precious in the sight of God. (v. 4)

Peter says that external beauty is ephemeral, but internal beauty is eternal. The one is attractive to the world; the other, to God. Peter describes this inner beauty as "a gentle and quiet spirit." It

---

3. The Greek term for *observe* in verse 2 suggests a careful observation, not a casual one.

might be paraphrased, "a gentle tranquility." Without question, this is a woman's most powerful quality—true character.

Evaluate Your Attention

> For in this way in former times the holy women also, who hoped in God, used to adorn themselves, being submissive to their own husbands. Thus Sarah obeyed Abraham, calling him lord,[4] and you have become her children if you do what is right without being frightened by any fear. (vv. 5–6)

The fact that Sarah called her husband her lord reveals volumes about their relationship. It shows that she respected him, was attentive to his needs, cooperated with his wishes, and adapted herself to his desires.

Wives, are you patterning yourself after Sarah's role model? Take a look at where you place most of your attention, where you spend your time, what the focus of your prayer life is. Is your husband at the top of your list, like Abraham was for Sarah?

Strong Commands to Husbands

The final verse in our passage for today turns the spotlight on the husband. It's short, but it's packed with three strong imperatives.

> You husbands likewise, live with your wives in an understanding way, as with a weaker vessel, since she is a woman; and grant her honor as a fellow heir of the grace of life. (v. 7a)

First: *Live with your wife.* The Greek term for live is a compound word composed of *sun* and *oikeō*, meaning "to dwell together" or to be "at home with." Peter is telling husbands here that they are responsible for the "close togetherness" in the relationship. Providing a good living should never become a substitute for sharing deeply in life. The husband should understand every room in his wife's heart and be sensitive to her needs.

Second: *Know your wife.* The husband is exhorted to live with his wife "in an understanding way." The phrase literally means, "according to knowledge." This doesn't refer to an academic knowledge of her, but to a deep understanding of how she is put together.

4. See Genesis 18:12.

It involves perceiving her innermost make-up, discerning her deepseated concerns and fears, and helping her work through them in the safety and security of your love. To live with her in an understanding way means to respect a "weaker vessel."

> The woman is called the "weaker partner" (*skeuos*, lit., "vessel"); but this is not to be taken morally, spiritually, or intellectually. It simply means that the woman has less physical strength. The husband must recognize this difference and take it into account.[5]

Third: *Honor your wife.* To "grant her honor"[6] is to assign her a place of honor. Authors Gary Smalley and John Trent define this word in their book *The Gift of Honor.*

> In ancient writings, something of honor was something of substance (literally heavy), valuable, costly, even priceless. For Homer, the Greek scholar, "The greater the cost of the gift, the more the honor." . . .
> . . . Not only does it signify something or someone who is a priceless treasure, but it is also used for someone who occupies a highly respected position in our lives, someone high on our priority list.[7]

That's how husbands are to treat their wives, to honor them by assigning them the top priority on their list of human relationships . . . in their schedules . . . and most importantly, in their hearts.

A Promise to Both Partners

Verse 7 closes with a purpose clause.

So that your prayers may not be hindered.

The husband and wife have an added incentive to live together in harmony—an effective prayer life. And what a wonderful promise it is! Maybe this promise is enticing enough to motivate you to domestic harmony.

---

5. Edwin A. Blum, "1 Peter" in *The Expositor's Bible Commentary*, ed. Frank E. Gaebelein (Grand Rapids, Mich.: Zondervan Publishing House, Regency Reference Library, 1981), vol. 12, p. 237.

6. The same word translated "honor" in verse 7 is translated "precious" in 1:19.

7. Gary Smalley and John Trent, *The Gift of Honor* (Nashville, Tenn.: Thomas Nelson Publishers, 1987), pp. 23, 25–26.

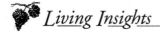 *Living Insights* STUDY ONE

Here are a couple of projects to help bring greater harmony to your marriage.

First, write down four qualities you appreciate most about your partner.

1. _____

_____

2. _____

_____

3. _____

_____

4. _____

_____

Now share them with your mate.

Second, using 1 Peter 3:1–7 as a guide, write down the one thing you would most like to change about yourself, and have your mate do the same.

You: _____

_____

Your mate: _____

_____

Be honest and vulnerable as you share these with each other.

 *Living Insights* STUDY TWO

Let's go back through our lesson and apply some of the counsel that Peter gives to husbands and wives.

We'll let the ladies go first. On a scale of one to ten, ten being Sarah, evaluate yourself in the categories on the following page.

Actions

Submissive	1	2	3	4	5	6	7	8	9	10
Chaste	1	2	3	4	5	6	7	8	9	10
Respectful	1	2	3	4	5	6	7	8	9	10

Adornment

Balance	1	2	3	4	5	6	7	8	9	10
Perspective	1	2	3	4	5	6	7	8	9	10

Attitude

Gentle	1	2	3	4	5	6	7	8	9	10
Quiet	1	2	3	4	5	6	7	8	9	10

Attention

Attentive	1	2	3	4	5	6	7	8	9	10
Cooperative	1	2	3	4	5	6	7	8	9	10
Adaptable	1	2	3	4	5	6	7	8	9	10

Women, for an insightful study in understanding and loving your husband, get a copy of Gary Smalley's *For Better or for Best*.

Now let's shift our focus onto the husband.

How close are you with your wife?

1 2 3 4 5 6 7 8 9 10

How understanding are you of her?

1 2 3 4 5 6 7 8 9 10

How well do you honor her?

1 2 3 4 5 6 7 8 9 10

Men, for a valuable guide to knowing, understanding, and loving your wife, pick up a copy of *If Only He Knew*, also by Gary Smalley.

Chapter 8

MATURITY CHECKPOINTS
1 Peter 3:8–12

En route to maturity, we all spill our milk, say things we shouldn't, and at times, don't act our age. At times we act like a two-year-old throwing a temper tantrum. At other times we pout like a pubescent child. Still other times we go through sweeping mood swings like an awkwardly adjusting teenager.

This process is called "growing up." And it's a painful one. We struggle through it more by trial and error than we do by unfaltering, charm-school grace. Consequently, every now and then we skin an elbow, bruise a knee, or bloody a nose from falling on our faces.

Growing up. Sooner or later we all have to do it. And the sooner we do, the easier it will be to walk the uneven and sometimes uncertain sidewalks of faith.

A Stated Goal for All God's Children

Growing up is a stated objective for all of God's family.

> For though by this time you ought to be teachers, you have need again for someone to teach you the elementary principles of the oracles of God, and you have come to need milk and not solid food. For everyone who partakes only of milk is not accustomed to the word of righteousness, for he is a babe. But solid food is for the mature, who because of practice have their senses trained to discern good and evil.
>
> Therefore leaving the elementary teaching about the Christ, *let us press on to maturity*, not laying again a foundation of repentance from dead works and of faith toward God, of instruction about washings, and laying on of hands, and the resurrection of the dead, and eternal judgment. (Heb. 5:12–6:2, emphasis added)

The problem the writer to the Hebrews addressed was a lack of maturity on the part of his readers. They had grown older in the faith, but they had not yet grown up. When they should have been building on the foundation laid by the apostles, they were playing blocks instead. They should have been digging their steak knives into a hunk of red meat, when in fact, they were still being bottle-fed milk.

To these slow growers, the writer gives two pieces of advice. First, *leave behind elementary teachings*—the matters of the sacrificial system, the basic pictures of Christ in the Old Testament, the gradeschool curriculum of truth (6:1–2). Second, *press on to maturity* (v. 1).

Few things are more pathetic than a person who has known the Lord for years, yet is still unable to feed on the Word of God without relying on others; someone who can't stand and walk but must toddle around steadied by someone else; someone who has grown old but who hasn't grown up.

Checkpoints That Reveal Maturity's Progress

First Peter 3 provides a yardstick for spiritual growth, a tangible, objective set of checkpoints we can all use to measure our maturity. The preceding context deals with specific instructions to Christians living in a secular society (2:11), to Christians facing a secular government (2:13), to Christians who are servants (2:18), to Christian wives who are married to unfair husbands (3:1), to Christian husbands (3:7). Beginning in verse 8, Peter summarizes his comments and, in doing so, sets forth eight checkpoints for maturity.

Unity

To sum up, let all be harmonious. (v. 8)

The first checkpoint is unity: "let all be harmonious." This quality refers to a oneness of heart, a similarity of purpose, and an agreement on major points of doctrine. It is not the same as *uniformity*, where there is a similarity in appearance or in thinking. It is not the same as *unanimity*, where there is 100 percent agreement. And it is not the same as *union*, where there is an affiliation with others but no common bond that makes them one at heart.

The secret to this kind of harmony is not to focus on petty, peripheral differences, but to focus on the common ground of Jesus and His kingdom (see Phil. 1:27).

Mutual Interest

Let all be . . . sympathetic. (1 Pet. 3:8)

The second checkpoint is mutual interest or, literally, "fellow feelings." The Greek root gives us our word *sympathy*, meaning "to feel with." This means that when others weep, you weep; when they rejoice, you rejoice (Rom. 12:15). It connotes the absence of competition or jealousy or envy with a fellow Christian (see also 1 Cor. 12:26).

Friendship and Affection

Let all be . . . brotherly. (1 Pet. 3:8)

The third checkpoint is friendship and affection. The word translated here as "brotherly" is from the Greek word *philos*. It has in mind the love of an affectionate friend. Coleridge once wrote of friendship as a "sheltering tree." When you have this quality, your branches reach out over the lives of others to give them shelter, shade, rest, relief, and encouragement.

Compassion

Let all be . . . kindhearted. (v. 8)

The fourth checkpoint is compassion. The Greek term means "kindhearted." It is used most often in the Gospels to describe Jesus. As a good shepherd, Jesus looked at humanity's lost sheep who were scattered, frightened, and hungry. What He saw pulled at His heartstrings (Matt. 9:36). Just as these hurting people touched the heart of Jesus, so should they touch our hearts. If they do, it's a definite checkpoint of spiritual growth.

Humility

Let all be . . . humble in spirit. (1 Pet. 3:8)

The fifth checkpoint is humility. The phrase "humble in spirit" is an internal attitude rather than external appearance, meaning "lowly" or "bowed down" in mind. In our day of spotlighting celebrities of the faith and magnifying the flesh, this quality is a rare commodity and is greatly valued by the Lord Jesus (see Matt. 6:1–4). All of verse 8 has been about how we should think and feel. In verses 9 through 11 Peter writes about what we should do and say, rounding out our checklist with these last three qualities.

Forgiveness

. . . not returning evil for evil, or insult for insult, but giving a blessing instead; for you were called for the very purpose that you might inherit a blessing. (v. 9)

Verse 9 touches all the important bases regarding forgiveness: refusing to get back or get even, restraining from saying anything ugly in return, returning good for evil, and keeping in mind that we were called to endure such harsh treatment (see 2:20–21). Whenever the urge to get even comes over you, it's important to realize that retaliation is a sign of adolescence, while restraint is a mark of maturity.

A Controlled Tongue

> "Let him who means to love life and see good days
> Refrain his tongue from evil and his lips from speaking guile." (3:10)

Peter is quoting from Psalm 34:12–16 in this verse and in verses 11 and 12. Here he says to "refrain" your tongue from evil; the psalmist used a little more forceful language: "Keep your tongue from evil." The idea is to get control of it, or as James says, put a bridle on it and hold it back from galloping headlong into evil (see James 3:1–10).

Notice again the beginning of 1 Peter 3:10—"Let him who means to love life and see good days . . ." A major way to accomplish that goal is to learn to control the tongue. People who have learned to restrain from gossip, from telling confidential information, and from passing on an unverified comment are people who are not only maturing but people who are enhancing the quality of their lives.

Purity and Peace

> "And let him turn away from evil and do good;
> Let him seek peace and pursue it." (v. 11)

The final checkpoint is *purity and peace.* Once we have pulled in the reins on our tongue, we are to spur ourselves on to purity and peace. Why? Verse 12 gives the answer.

> "For the eyes of the Lord are upon the righteous,
> And His ears attend to their prayer."

The eyes and ears of the Lord are emblematic of God's providential care for His people (see Exod. 2:25; 3:7). Regarding that thought is a beautiful verse tucked away in 2 Chronicles 16:9a.

"For the eyes of the Lord move to and fro throughout the earth that He may strongly support those whose heart is completely His."

What a wonderful reason for pursuing purity and peace—the promise of God's providential care!

That's quite a checklist, isn't it? Eight distinct notches to mark our Christian maturity. How do you measure up when you stand under that list?

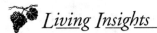 *Living Insights*

The call for the Christian to "grow up" reverberates loud and clear throughout the Scriptures. Ephesians 4:15–16 is just one echo.

> But speaking the truth in love, we are to grow up in all aspects into Him, who is the head, even Christ, from whom the whole body, being fitted and held together by that which every joint supplies, according to the proper working of each individual part, causes the growth of the body for the building up of itself in love.

From this passage, jot down every observation you can about growing up in Christ.

_____

_____

_____

_____

_____

_____

_____

_____

_____

_____

_____

What is an integral factor to our spiritual growth (see 1 Pet. 2:2)?

_____

Who is *immediately* responsible for our growth (see 1 Cor. 3:5– 7)?

_____

Who is *ultimately* responsible (see 1 Cor. 3:6)?

_____

From 1 Corinthians 3:1–17, what metaphors does Paul use to describe the process of growth?

1. _____

2. _____

3. _____

What observations about your own spiritual growth can you derive from these metaphors?

Metaphor 1:_____

_____

Metaphor 2:_____

_____

Metaphor 3:_____

_____

🍇 *Living Insights* _____ STUDY TWO

Let's take a few minutes to place ourselves under the yardstick of 1 Peter 3:8–12 to measure our growth toward Christian maturity. How would you evaluate yourself in the following areas? Circle your progress.

Promoting Unity	toddler	child	adolescent	adult
Interest in Others	toddler	child	adolescent	adult
Friendship and Affection	toddler	child	adolescent	adult

Compassion	toddler	child	adolescent	adult
Humility	toddler	child	adolescent	adult
Forgiveness	toddler	child	adolescent	adult
Controlled Tongue	toddler	child	adolescent	adult
Purity and Peace	toddler	child	adolescent	adult

In which area are you least mature? _____

What could you do to "grow up" in that area?

_____

_____

_____

_____

_____

_____

Chapter 9

WHEN LIFE "JUST AIN'T FAIR"

1 Peter 3:13–17

An old French fairy tale tells the story of two daughters—one bad and the other good, with the bad daughter being loved by the mother and the good one being unjustly despised and abused.

One day, while drawing water from a far-off well, the good daughter met a poor woman who asked if the little girl would give her a drink of water. "Ay, with all my heart," the kind girl responded as she helped her get a drink. The woman, who was a fairy in disguise, was so pleased with the kindness and good manners of the girl that she gave her a gift: every time the good daughter would speak, a flower or jewel would come out of her mouth.

When the little girl got home, her mother began to scold her for taking so long. But when the daughter started to apologize, two roses, two pearls, and two diamonds came out of her mouth. Her mother was astonished. After hearing her daughter's story and seeing an immeasurable number of diamonds come out in the telling, the mother called her other daughter and sent her to get the same gift. This favored daughter, however, was reluctant to be seen performing the lowly task of drawing water, so she went grumbling sourly all the way to the well. When she got there, a beautiful, queenly woman—that same fairy in disguise again—came to her and asked for a drink. Disagreeable and proud, the girl responded rudely. As a result, she received for her reward the "gift" of emitting snakes and toads every time she opened her mouth.[1]

How's that for poetic justice!

There's something in each one of us that longs for circumstances to be fair, isn't there? Maybe that's why fairy tales are so appealing. Good people are not long in receiving their rewards, and bad people are swiftly and soundly punished. Life works out, and everyone lives happily ever after.

Unfortunately, real life doesn't always turn out that way. As

---

1. "Toads and Diamonds" in *The Riverside Anthology of Children's Literature*, 6th ed. (Boston, Mass.: Houghton Mifflin Co., 1985), pp. 292–93.

author M. Scott Peck succinctly states: "Life is difficult."[2]

As Christians, we know that, ultimately, good will triumph over evil and that our God is just and kind and fair. But what can we do with the injustices and unfairnesses in the meantime? How can we keep pressing on during those times when life "just ain't fair"? Let's turn to 1 Peter 3:13–17 and see what we can learn from Peter's words to the suffering and persecuted first-century Christians.

Two Different and Distinct Perspectives

Our response to unfairness, as in all other issues, is based on our perspective—the particular vantage point from which we look at life. Basically, we have two perspectives to choose from: the human perspective or the divine.

The Human Perspective

Our natural, human perspective contends that since life isn't fair, we're going to get our share; we're going to look out for number one and not get mad but get even. Unfortunately, although we may succeed in getting even, peace will still elude us. We're more likely to reach the end of our lives as bitter, cynical, hostile people if our response to unfairness springs only from this perspective.

The Divine Perspective

We do have another option, however, and it's found in 1 Peter 3:12.

> "For the eyes of the Lord are upon the righteous,
> And His ears attend to their prayer,
> But the face of the Lord is against those who do
> evil."

The principle that Peter is giving us is this: God misses nothing. He's looking out for us, He's listening to our prayers, and He is completely aware of the evil that is happening to us.

But if this is true, we wonder, why doesn't He do something about the evil? Why does He let it go on so long? Because God's time line is infinite—He doesn't close His books at the end of each month. It may take a lifetime—or longer—before justice is served. But we can count on the fact that in the end God will be just. In

---

2. M. Scott Peck, *The Road Less Traveled* (New York, N.Y.: Simon and Schuster, A Touchstone Book, 1978), p. 15.

the end, everything will "work together for good" (Rom. 8:28).

Some Helpful and Insightful Techniques

Building on this divine perspective, Peter gives us five ways we can live in an unfair and inequitable world. But first there's a general principle we need to be aware of.

General Principle

This principle is found in 1 Peter 3:13.

> And who is there to harm you if you prove zealous for what is good?

If we were to paraphrase this verse, we could say that those who live honest lives will usually not suffer harm. *Usually.* There are exceptions to most every rule, as we'll see in the rest of today's passage. But as a general rule, if you live a clean and honest life, you usually won't suffer for it.

For example, if you pay your debts, chances are good that you won't get into financial trouble. If you take care of your body, chances are good that you will live a healthier life than those who don't. If you help others in need, chances are good that when you are in need someone will be there to help you out.

Occasional Inequities

However, we've all experienced those rare occasions when life "just ain't fair." And it's these exceptions to the rule[3] for which Peter suggests five responses in verses 14–17.

First: *Consider yourself uniquely blessed by God.*

> But even if you should suffer for the sake of righteousness, you are blessed. (v. 14a)

---

3. We know that unjust suffering is an exception to the rule because of the particular nuance of the word *if.* In Greek, there were four ways or conditions to use the word *if*: the first-class condition, meaning "assumed as true," which was a very common usage (see Matt. 4:3, 6); the second-class condition, meaning "assumed as not true," also a common usage (see Gal. 1:10); the third-class condition, meaning "maybe, maybe not," also common (see 1 Pet. 3:13); and the fourth-class condition, meaning "unlikely but possible." This last condition is rarely used in Scripture, but this is the condition Peter used in verse 14, which could be reworded as: "It is unlikely that you should suffer for the sake of righteousness, but if you should . . . " This same conditional use is also found in verse 17.

As far as the injustice itself is concerned, Peter's surprising advice is, "Be happy! Consider yourself blessed!" James also tells us something similar in the first chapter of his letter.

> When all kinds of trials and temptations crowd into your lives, my brothers, don't resent them as intruders, but welcome them as friends! (James 1:2 PHILLIPS)

This sure sounds nice, but really, how can we be happy and consider ourselves blessed when we've just been punched in the eye with the fist of injustice? We can do this by remembering two things: first, we are called to patiently endure unfair treatment (see 1 Pet. 2:21; 3:9) so that when it comes we can know we're still experiencing God's plan and fulfilling our calling; and second, someday we will be rewarded for our endurance of these undeserved trials (see Matt. 5:10–12; James 1:12).

Because of these two promises, Christians can do something different from all the rest of humanity: we can respond to injustice with a positive attitude.

Second: *Don't panic and don't worry.*

> And do not fear their intimidation, and do not be troubled. (1 Pet. 3:14b)

The word fear comes from the Greek *phobos*, from which we get our word *phobia*. This fear refers to "being seized with terror and running, taking flight." In this first phrase Peter is telling us not to run away from the trial, not to panic. In the second phrase he says that we don't need to "be troubled." The word *troubled* in Greek means "to be agitated, uneasy"; it signifies inner agitation (see also John 14:1).

Peter's counsel to us is that, even when trials are pressing in and people are trying to intimidate us, we can have a calmness of spirit. We can be free from inner agitation and worry because we know that God is on our side.

Third: *Acknowledge Christ as Lord even over this event.*

> But sanctify Christ as Lord in your hearts. (1 Pet. 3:15a)

A good example of someone who sanctified the Lord is Stephen. After giving an eloquent and penetrating defense of Jesus before the Jewish council, Stephen was stoned to death by the enraged

Jews. Let's look back at the last few moments of his life.

> Now when they heard this, they were cut to the quick, and they began gnashing their teeth at him. But being full of the Holy Spirit, he gazed intently into heaven and saw the glory of God, and Jesus standing at the right hand of God; and he said, "Behold, I see the heavens opened up and the Son of Man standing at the right hand of God." But they cried out with a loud voice, and covered their ears, and they rushed upon him with one impulse. And when they had driven him out of the city, they began stoning him, and the witnesses laid aside their robes at the feet of a young man named Saul. And they went on stoning Stephen as he called upon the Lord and said, "Lord Jesus, receive my spirit!" And falling on his knees, he cried out with a loud voice, "Lord, do not hold this sin against them!" And having said this, he fell asleep. (Acts 7:54–60)

Such a savage and undeserved attack! But when those men looked into Stephen's face, they didn't find their own hatred reflected back at them—they saw the reflection of the Savior's grace and love. Stephen could have died with bitterness and cursing on his lips, but instead he uttered a prayer of forgiveness for those who had so mercilessly mistreated him.

Like Stephen, we need to acknowledge Christ's control over our unfair circumstances and do our best to see that He is glorified in them.

Fourth: *Be ready to give a witness.*

> Always being ready to make a defense to everyone who asks you to give an account for the hope that is in you, yet with gentleness and reverence. (1 Pet. 3:15b)

William Barclay explains what our "defense" and "account" should be like.

> It must be *reasonable.* It is a *logos* that the Christian must give, and a *logos* is a reasonable and intelligent statement of his position. . . . To do so we must know what we believe; we must have thought

it out; we must be able to state it intelligently and intelligibly. . . .

His defence must be given with *gentleness*. . . . The case for Christianity must be presented with winsomeness and with love. . . . Men may be wooed into the Christian faith when they cannot be bullied into it.

His defence must be given *with reverence*. That is to say, any argument in which the Christian is involved must be carried on in a tone which God can hear with joy. . . . In any presentation of the Christian case and in any argument for the Christian faith, the accent should be the accent of love.[4]

Seldom will there be a more opportune time to share about God than when you are suffering and glorifying Him through it.

Fifth: *Keep a good conscience.*

And keep a good conscience so that in the thing in which you are slandered, those who revile your good behavior in Christ may be put to shame. (v. 16)

Here Peter digs below the surface, turning up the rich soil of inner character. And what is the prize he is trying to unearth? *Integrity.* There is nothing more powerful, there is no more eloquent defense, than a life continually lived in integrity. It alone has the power to silence your slanderers.

The Underlying and Unwavering Principle

Peter's conclusion in verse 17 brings us full circle.

For it is better, if God should will it so, that you suffer for doing what is right rather than for doing what is wrong.

Simply stated, the principle is this: unjust suffering is always better than deserved punishment. And sometimes—we can't always explain why—it is God's will that we should suffer for doing what is right.

---

4. William Barclay, *The Letters of James and Peter*, rev. ed., The Daily Study Bible Series (Philadelphia, Pa.: Westminster Press, 1976), pp. 230–31.

An old Hebrew tale tells the story of a righteous man who suffered undeservedly. He was a man who had turned away from evil, taken care of his family, walked with God, and been renowned for his integrity. But in a few moments' span, he lost everything he had: his flocks, his cattle, his servants, his children, and finally his health. This old Hebrew story is no fairy tale. It is the story of a real person—Job.

But though he suffered terribly, today he is counted as blessed because of his patient endurance.

> Behold, we count those blessed who endured. You have heard of the endurance of Job and have seen the outcome of the Lord's dealings, that the Lord is full of compassion and is merciful. (James 5:11)

If God has called you to be a Job—and this is a rare calling—remember that the Lord is not only full of compassion but is fully in control. And He will not leave you without hope. In Proverbs 16:7 He promises:

> When a man's ways are pleasing to the Lord,
> He makes even his enemies to be at peace with him.

 Pro 16:7

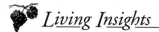 *Living Insights*

One of the responses to unjust suffering that Peter wants us to have is to be ready to give a witness. Many of us, however, when put on the spot, either go absolutely blank or stammer over a few nervously formed words.

Let's use our time today to put together, as William Barclay phrased it, "a reasonable and intelligent" explanation for the hope within us.

In a few concise statements, write down the key thoughts you would want to share with someone who asked you about your beliefs.

_____

_____

_____

_____

_____

_____

_____

_____

_____

_____

_____

_____

_____

   Next, take those statements and fashion them into an articulate paragraph that feels natural to the way you speak.

_____

_____

_____

_____

_____

_____

_____

_____

_____

_____

_____

_____

_____

Now practice saying this until you're comfortable with it. The purpose of this exercise is not to memorize a pat answer, but to clarify your thoughts and more easily communicate a brief, relaxed testimony.

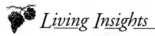 *Living Insights* _____ STUDY TWO

Another response we should have is to acknowledge Christ as Lord even when enduring unjust suffering. Sometimes it's hard to know exactly how to do that, especially when we're hurting. But one good way is through prayer. If you are struggling to find the right words to say, why don't you let the following prayer be a guide for you.

> Dear Father,
>
> Something has happened to me that I don't deserve. I haven't done anything wrong, yet wrong has been done against me.
>
> I'm so glad You're with me right now. You are here, and You have Your reasons for allowing this to happen. I know You will not take advantage of me. You will not let this go any further than what pleases You. You're much too kind to be cruel, and You're much too good to be unjust.
>
> Please take charge of this situation, Lord. Use my integrity to defend me. Give me the grace to stay calm. And please take control of my emotions.
>
> Lord, it seems that there is no way I can set the record straight, and it's getting tougher to cope. I find myself cast at Your disposal. You be the sovereign; You be the master over this moment. Because I can't change this person, and I can't alter this event, please, Father, You be the Lord over it.
>
> For Jesus' sake, Amen.

Chapter 10

CRUCIFIXION, PROCLAMATION, RESURRECTION, EXALTATION

1 Peter 3:18–22

Are you familiar with the Apostles' Creed?
I believe in God the Father Almighty, maker of
heaven and earth;
And in Jesus Christ, His only begotten Son, our
Lord, who was conceived by the Holy Ghost, born
of the Virgin Mary, suffered under Pontius Pilate,
was crucified, dead and buried; He descended into
hell; the third day He rose again from the dead; He
ascended into heaven, and sitteth at the right hand
of God the Father Almighty; from thence He shall
come to judge the quick and the dead.
I believe in the Holy Spirit, the holy catholic[1]
church, the communion of saints, the forgiveness of
sins, the resurrection of the body, and the life ever-
lasting. Amen.[2]

A beautiful statement of the essential truths of our faith, eloquent in its simplicity. But though the words are simple, the concepts are by no means simplistic. One of the most difficult concepts
communicated in this creed is found in the words, "He descended
into hell."

These words have their root in 1 Peter 3:19, the most troublesome section in Peter's entire first letter—in fact, one of the thorn-
iest in the whole New Testament. And it's this particular verse that
is at the center of our passage for today.

General Observations of the Paragraph

As a general principle, it's helpful to get an overview of the

---

1. The word *catholic* is used here to mean "universal"—"I believe in the universal church"—
rather than the Roman Catholic Church. The word *Christian* is often substituted for it.

2. The Apostles' Creed, quoted in *Great Hymns of the Faith* (Grand Rapids, Mich.: Singspi-
ration, Zondervan Publishing House, 1968), p. 492.

context of a troublesome passage before digging into it. And that's what we want to do now.

If we stand back to get the whole picture of verses 18–22, we can make at least three observations that will help us understand Peter's difficult words in verses 19 and 21.

First, though the verses we are looking at appear at the end of a chapter, they are actually in the middle of a paragraph. Beginning at verse 13 of chapter 3, this paragraph extends all the way through verse 6 of chapter 4. As with most paragraphs, there is a main subject that holds the author's thoughts together. The subject for this particular paragraph is unjust suffering, best stated in 3:17.

> For it is better, if God should will it so, that you
> suffer for doing what is right rather than for doing
> what is wrong.

Peter takes this broad subject and distills it into one main point: blessings follow suffering for well-doing. This point makes the old disciple think of the one man who illustrated it best—his beloved Master, Jesus.

Which brings us to our second observation: Jesus alone is the focal point of verses 18–22. In verse 18, we see His crucifixion; in verse 19, His proclamation; in verse 21, His resurrection; and in verse 22, His exaltation.

So far, Peter's train of thought seems to be following a logical progression. But as we get further into verse 19, we see that he has veered off in another direction. Our third observation, then, is that this passage contains a digression. And the two knotty issues that emerge from this detour are Christ's descent "into hell" and the baptism that "now saves you" (vv. 19–21).

But before we try to untangle these two knotty issues, let's isolate the central thread that forms the theme to our passage.

Central Theme of the Passage

This theme intertwines itself around three difficult verses. The first is verse 18.

> For Christ also died for sins once for all, the just for
> the unjust, in order that He might bring us to God,
> having been put to death in the flesh, but made alive
> in the spirit.

This verse encapsulates the gospel in the briefest of terms. Here Peter reiterates that Christ died to solve the sin problem, that His death was a once-for-all transaction, and that it accomplished its purpose—the One who was just died for the many who were unjust so that He might bring us to God.

Christ provides us with an entrée to God; He has given us immediate and permanent access to our heavenly Father. So the next time you wonder if unjust suffering can ultimately bring bless- ing, remember the Cross. That is its message.

Now, if we drop down to the thread of verse 22, we see that the focus is still on Christ.

> Who is at the right hand of God, having gone into heaven, after angels and authorities and powers had been subjected to Him.

This verse tells us what Christ is doing today. After ascending from this earth, He went back to the place of glory—the right hand of God. There He sits and makes intercession for us, as He is moved by our needs and infirmities. From the place of highest authority He watches over us, waiting for the day that He will return to the earth to judge the living and the dead.

Christ, then, is the central theme of this passage. Now let's move on to the tough part.

A Critical Analysis of the Problems

The first of our two problems is found in verses 19–20.

> In which also He went and made proclamation to the spirits now in prison, who once were disobedi- ent, when the patience of God kept waiting in the days of Noah, during the construction of the ark, in which a few, that is, eight persons, were brought safely through the water.

Let's begin unraveling the meaning of this verse by first deter- mining who these "spirits" are.[3] If you turn back a few pages in time, back to the days before the flood, you'll find yourself at the

---

3. For the three main interpretations of this verse, consult Edwin A. Blum, "1 Peter," *The Expositor's Bible Commentary*, ed. Frank E. Gaebelein (Grand Rapids, Mich.: Zondervan Publishing House, Regency Reference Library, 1981), vol. 12, p. 241.

start of Genesis, chapter 6. In the first six verses, you'll stumble upon a scene of such great depravity that when God saw it, He was literally "grieved in His heart" (v. 6).

It seems that there was some kind of intercourse, many believe sexual intercourse, between spirit beings and women during this time of earth's history. These spirit beings were most likely fallen angels (see Jude 6), and their heinous lifestyle was wiped out with the judgment of the flood.

However, they were not drowned but were incarcerated instead. In the original language this place of incarceration is called Tartarus, and Peter here calls it "prison" (compare 2 Pet. 2:4). It is not hell but a kind of death-row holding cell. There they await the final day of judgment when they will be cast with Satan into the lake of fire, the place originally created for him and his demons.

OK. We've seen what the "spirits" and the "prison" are, now what about this "proclamation"? What kind of a proclamation would Christ make to fallen angels? If we look at the word *proclamation* in Greek, we find the word *kērussō*, a term for declaring an edict or heralding an announcement. It is not the word for declaring the gospel, so we can infer that Christ was not ministering or witnessing to the wicked spirits.

Rather, after Christ died and His body was placed in the grave, His spirit descended into the bowels of the earth to Tartarus. There He proclaimed His victory over death, over sin, and over the power of Satan. This proclamation caused the demons to realize that their work had been in vain, and that all of their attempts to sabotage our salvation through the Cross were nullified.

So far we've focused on the problem of verse 19. Now let's explore verse 20, which is kind of a prelude to the second troublesome issue found in verse 21.

> When the patience of God kept waiting in the days of Noah, during the construction of the ark, in which a few, that is, eight persons, were brought safely through the water. (v. 20)

Those eight in Noah's family were the only people of all the millions who lived in that era to make it through the Flood. It was because of the ark that Noah and his family "were brought safely through the water."

Here Peter is highlighting the symbolic significance of the Flood for the believer. The flood waters were waters of death that buried the people in a watery grave. But, and don't miss this now, *these same waters that swallowed up the earth in judgment and death lifted the eight who were in the ark to safety.* It's a vivid picture of our salvation.[4]

Today we have another vivid and lovely picture of salvation: baptism. The water of baptism, like the flood waters in ancient days, pictures death. As we go down into that water, we illustrate our death to sin and our burial with Christ. As we rise up out of the water, we illustrate our resurrection to a new kind of life (see Rom. 6:1–4).

Which brings us to the second of Peter's problematic statements, found in verse 21.

> And corresponding to that, baptism now saves you —not the removal of dirt from the flesh, but an appeal to God for a good conscience—through the resurrection of Jesus Christ.

The thread that we need to pull to unravel this knotty statement is in the phrase, "And corresponding to that." Corresponding to what? To what Peter has just been talking about in the previous verse—the symbolic picture of the ark. In other words, Peter is saying, "As the waters in Noah's day lifted up the ark and gave safety to those within, so the waters of baptism today symbolize salvation to those who are baptized."

The act of baptism doesn't save us, it just symbolizes the salvation that has already taken place. Peter himself clearly states that those baptismal waters in no way cleanse the flesh—either literally or figuratively—but they do give us a good conscience toward God. The Living Bible does a fine job of clarifying this.

> That, by the way, is what baptism pictures for us: In baptism we show that we have been saved from death and doom by the resurrection of Christ; not because our bodies are washed clean by the water, but because in being baptized we are turning to God and asking him to cleanse our hearts from sin. (v. 21 TLB)

---

4. "Water was the means for destroying all the rest; that same water was the means for floating the ark with its eight souls. Water was a means of judgment in the case of those, a means of saving in the case of these. We may add that Christ also has the same effect upon men (Luke 2:34); the Christ whom the damned saw in terror in hell is the same Christ who is our hope in heaven." R. C. H. Lenski, *The Interpretation of the Epistles of St. Peter, St. John and St. Jude* (Columbus, Ohio: Wartburg Press, 1945), p. 169.

Practical Reminder of the Principles

As we conclude our thoughts on these problematic verses from Peter's pen, two pragmatic principles emerge.

First: *When unjust suffering seems unbearable, remember the Cross.* When we start thinking about how terribly unjust our suffering is —and it may very well be—we will find comfort in the love of Him

> who, although He existed in the form of God, did not regard equality with God a thing to be grasped, but emptied Himself, taking the form of a bondservant, and being made in the likeness of men. And being found in appearance as a man, He humbled Himself by becoming obedient to the point of death, even death on a cross. (Phil. 2:6–8)

Christ knows our sufferings and pain and, because of His love, has entered into them with us (Heb. 4:15; John 3:16; 15:13–15).

Second: *When the fear of death steals your peace, remember the Resurrection.* Meditate on the tender and exultant words of the hymnist:

> I know that my Redeemer lives:
> What joy the blest assurance gives!
> He lives, He lives, who once was dead;
> He lives, my everlasting Head!
>
> He lives, to bless me with His love;
> He lives to plead for me above;
> He lives, my hungry soul to feed;
> He lives, to help in time of need.
>
> He lives, and grants me daily breath;
> He lives, and I shall conquer death;
> He lives, my future to prepare;
> He lives, to bring me safely there.
>
> He lives, all glory to His Name;
> He lives, My Savior, still the same;

What joy the blest assurance gives:
I know that my Redeemer lives![5]

"I believe in God the Father Almighty, maker of heaven and earth; And in Jesus Christ, His only begotten Son, our Lord, who . . . was crucified, dead and buried; He descended into hell; the third day He rose again from the dead . . ." Each of the statements in the Apostles' Creed is a priceless heirloom, carefully handed down through the church from generation to generation. But the most important part of this creed is the phrase, "I believe." That simple but sincere statement of faith makes all the difference in this world . . . and the next.

Living Insights

A creed is often helpful in crystallizing your beliefs. Try putting what you believe into words, using the Apostles' Creed as a model or creating a form of your own. Include only those elements of your faith that you consider essential.

_____

_____

_____

_____

_____

_____

_____

_____

_____

_____

_____

_____

5. Samuel Medley, "I Know That My Redeemer Lives," *Hymns for the Family of God* (Nashville, Tenn.: Paragon Associates, 1976), no. 295.

Now write a creed not of your beliefs but of your behavior. From that statement of faith, tell how your beliefs have changed the way you live, the way you feel, the way you look at life, etc.

_____

_____

_____

_____

_____

_____

_____

_____

_____

_____

Food for thought: James 2:14–26.

🍇 *Living Insights*   STUDY TWO

The ascension of Christ is a little-studied doctrine, but one that has far-reaching applications for the believer. Look up the following passages and note some of the ways Jesus' ascension affects you today.

John 14:2 _____

_____

John 14:16 _____

_____

Romans 8:34 _____

_____

2 Corinthians 5:1–8 _____

_____

Ephesians 4:8–12 _____

_____

Hebrews 4:14–16 _____

_____

Hebrews 6:19–20 _____

_____

Hebrews 9:24_____

_____

Hebrews 12:1–3 _____

_____

Now use your answers to form a prayer list and thank the Lord Jesus, focusing not so much on what He has done for you, but on what He is *presently* doing.

Chapter 11

HOW TO SHOCK
THE PAGAN CROWD
1 Peter 4:1–6

When American soldiers occupied western Europe during the Second World War, they were uprooted from their homeland and, for a temporary time, transplanted onto foreign soil. The Europeans who observed these men had their perception of America shaped by the behavior they saw them exhibit.

Sadly, for many, that perception wasn't good. American soldiers overseas often viewed their weekend pass as a license to unbutton their collars and let their desires run riot in the streets and taverns. It's no wonder the term "ugly American" emerged as a label for such men.

As Christians, we face a similar situation. Since our citizenship is in heaven, the earth is really not our home. For us, it is foreign soil. Consequently, we need to be on our best behavior, otherwise people will get a distorted perception of what our homeland is like. As a result of our behavior, they will either be attracted to or repelled by heaven, the place we call home.

In 1 Peter 4:1–6, the apostle gives some marching orders to us Christian soldiers who are stationed on foreign soil.

Provisions: Dynamic Power of Christ's Death

Peter opens the subject of a Christian's behavior before a watching world with the causal connective *therefore*.

> Therefore, since Christ has suffered in the flesh,
> arm yourselves also with the same purpose.
> (1 Pet. 4:1a)

The word *therefore* is a word of summary that connects what the author is about to say with what he has just said. And what has he just said? Look back at 3:18 and 22. He has said that Christ has suffered and died on our behalf, the just for the unjust. Commentator Kenneth Wuest illuminates 4:1 with some interesting linguistic and historical background material.

> [Peter] exhorts the saints to arm themselves with the same mind that Christ had regarding unjust punishment. . . . The Greek word translated "arm yourselves" was used of a Greek soldier putting on his armor and taking his weapons. The noun of the same root was used of a heavy-armed footsoldier who carried a pike and a large shield. . . . The Christian needs the heaviest armor he can get to withstand the attacks of the enemy of his soul.[1]

This word picture offers a blunt reminder that we Christians are not living on this earth as tourists. We are not vacationing our way to heaven. We are soldiers. Everywhere around us the battle rages. The danger is real, and the enemy is formidable. Christ died not only to gain victory over sin's dominion but to equip us for that fight, to give us the inner equipment we need to stand against it.

Transformation: Remarkable Difference in the Christian Life

As a result of the relationship we have with our triumphant King, we soldiers share the victor's spoils. Verses 1b–3 catalog those rewards.

> Because he who has suffered in the flesh has ceased from sin, so as to live the rest of the time in the flesh no longer for the lusts of men, but for the will of God. For the time already past is sufficient for you to have carried out the desire of the Gentiles, having pursued a course of sensuality, lusts, drunkenness, carousals, drinking parties and abominable idolatries.

At least four benefits of our being "in Christ" are listed: One, *we no longer serve sin as our master* (v. 1b); two, *we don't spend our days overcome by desires as we once did* (v. 2a); three, *we now live for the will of God* (v. 2b); four, *we have closed the book on godless living* (v. 3).

Notice in these verses how the "will of God" (v. 2) is contrasted to "the desire of the Gentiles" (v. 3). Notice, too, how "the desire of the Gentiles"—the old habits, practices, associations, places of amusement, evil motives, and wicked pastimes—is all a part of the

---

1. Kenneth Wuest, *First Peter: In the Greek New Testament* (Grand Rapids, Mich.: William B. Eerdmans Publishing Co., 1942), p. 110.

past. Take a quick glance at all that Peter places into this category. *Sensuality*, which refers to actions that disgust and shock public decency. *Lusts*, which go beyond sexual promiscuity and include sinful desires of any kind. *Drunkenness, carousals*, and *drinking parties*, which portray a whole miserable spectrum of pleasure-seeking consumption, from wanton substance abuse to wild sexual orgies. What is so liberating about our relationship with Christ is that He fills the void in our life which we once tried to fill with all that garbage. With the void filled, the gnawing emptiness that went with it is gone too. And with the emptiness gone, we no longer crave the things we used to crave.

That's where Christians are different from the world. That's where we stand out. That's where the light shines in the darkness. But, invariably, the darkness reacts to such a light.

Reaction: Angry Astonishment from the Unsaved World

The reaction of your unsaved friends, convicted by the changes in your life, is warned of in verse 4.

> And in all this, they are surprised that you do not run with them into the same excess of dissipation, and they malign you.

The Living Bible makes the point more vividly.

> Of course, your former friends will be very surprised when you don't eagerly join them any more in the wicked things they do, and they will laugh at you in contempt and scorn.

Brace yourself for those reactions if you've just broken off from a wild bunch of friends and Jesus is transforming you. Your old friends will not only be shocked at your new lifestyle, they might actively ridicule and unjustly judge you for it as well.

The terrible irony of our unsaved friends' judgment is that they themselves will face the ultimate judgment.

> But they shall give account to Him who is ready to judge the living and the dead. (v. 5)

Ideally, we want to be a fragrant aroma of Christ in winsomely attracting the unsaved to Jesus. But Scripture, as well as our own experience, teaches us that what is fragrant to some is fetid to others.

Summation: Gospel Preached to the Physically Dead

The context of Peter's letter has to do with being mistreated and maligned, with being unjustly punished and persecuted. Sometimes that malicious mistreatment results in a believer's life not only being threatened but taken. That's what verse 6 has in mind.

> For the gospel has for this purpose been preached even to those who are dead, that though they are judged in the flesh as men, they may live in the spirit according to the will of God.

On this difficult verse Kenneth Wuest comments.

> The words, "[those who] are dead," refer to Christian believers who had died. The gospel had been preached to them and they had become Christians. As a result of this they had been judged according to men while they were on earth. This judgment was in the form of persecution because of their Christian testimony.
> . . . These Christians died, many of them as martyrs. . . . They in their disembodied state were serving the Lord in the future life.[2]

All believers owe it to themselves to read at least a portion of *Foxe's Book of Martyrs*. It traces the martyrdom of Christians throughout the centuries and demonstrates how darkly the world can act in its attempt to extinguish the light of Christlike character. Do you, like the brave saints of old, want to stand out like a bright light against the darkness of your world? Do you want to shock the pagan crowd? You don't need flamboyance or fanaticism. You don't need to wag your finger or rail against others' lifestyles. You simply need to live differently. And if you do, you need to be aware of the consequences of Christlike living. For some it may mean persecution; for others, it may mean even death . . . as it did for John Hus.

Prior to his appearance before the Council of Constance in 1414, Hus sent a letter to one of his friends in Bohemia.

> "I shall not be led astray by them to the side of evil, though I suffer at His will temptations, revilings,

---

2. Wuest, *First Peter: In the Greek New Testament*, p. 114.

89

imprisonments, and deaths—as indeed He too suffered, and hath subjected His loved servants to the same trials, leaving us an example that we may suffer for His sake and our salvation. If He suffered, being what He was, why should not we?"[3]

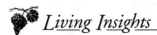 *Living Insights*

The passage for today instructed us that we should keep our eyes fixed on Christ, continue living for Him, and not be surprised when we are misunderstood or mistreated.

Look up the following verses and distill each of them down to a pocket principle that you can pull out when you need strength or encouragement.

Verses for Strength and Encouragement

Matthew 5:10–12 _____

_____

John 15:20 _____

_____

1 Peter 2:19–23_____

_____

1 Peter 4:14 _____

_____

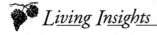 *Living Insights*

The writer to the Hebrews gives us some important instructions to anchor us when we find ourselves in the midst of a storm of persecution.

---

3. Quoted by John Moffat in *The General Epistles: James, Peter, and Judas* (London, England: Hodder and Stoughton, 1928), p. 147.

Therefore, since we have so great a cloud of witnesses surrounding us, let us also lay aside every encumbrance, and the sin which so easily entangles us, and let us run with endurance the race that is set before us, fixing our eyes on Jesus, the author and perfecter of faith, who for the joy set before Him endured the cross, despising the shame, and has sat down at the right hand of the throne of God. For consider Him who has endured such hostility by sinners against Himself, so that you may not grow weary and lose heart. (Heb. 12:1–3)

Write down your observations of this passage.

_____

_____

_____

_____

_____

_____

_____

_____

_____

_____

_____

_____

_____

_____

_____

_____

_____

_____

_____

Let's take a few minutes to do what the author of Hebrews instructs us to do—fix our eyes on Jesus and consider the hostility He endured. Next to each of these passages from Matthew's gospel, jot down the form of hostility Christ encountered.

12:14 _____

12:24 _____

26:59 _____

26:65–68 _____

27:27–31 _____

27:39–44 _____

After meditating on the hostilities Jesus faced, write down a few of the misunderstandings and mistreatments you have suffered from other people.

_____

_____

_____

_____

_____

_____

Now compare what you have suffered to what Jesus has suffered.

_____

_____

_____

_____

_____

_____

Chapter 12

FOUR COMMANDS...
ONE GOAL
1 Peter 4:7–11

Peter was a practical man. Being married helped. So did his
background as a fisherman. Prior to following Christ, his life
consisted of very tangible, practical things: boats, nets, fish, sup-
porting a family, hard work, competition, and a host of other realities. Consequently, we should not be surprised that his personality
and his prose follow suit.

Being neither scholarly nor sophisticated, Peter had little interest in theoretical discussions. Life was not meant to be talked
about but lived. If an urgent situation demanded action, Peter
wasn't one to call for a committee to study the alternatives. He cut
through the bureaucratic red tape and got down to business.

So when the big fisherman took up his pen to write about
suffering saints, he cut to the chase. And when he addressed the
reality of the end times, he summed up a game plan in a one-two-
three fashion rather than by waxing eloquent on the options. In
the five verses we will look at today, we see pragmatic Peter at his
best, as he offers four commands and one goal. Simple. Direct. No
beating around the bush.

A Few Reminders about End Times

Before we take a look at Peter's marching orders, let's review a
few things said by Jesus and Paul concerning the end times.

Jesus' Predictions

When Jesus was with the twelve disciples, He trained them and
taught them in a calm, deliberate manner. As they ate together. As
they ministered to the masses. As they talked with individuals. As
they confronted the scribes and Pharisees.

However, when the shadow of the Cross lengthened to fall
ominously across Jesus' path, that became the sole focus of His
attention.

From that time Jesus Christ began to show His

disciples that He must go to Jerusalem, and suffer many things from the elders and chief priests and scribes, and be killed, and be raised up on the third day. And Peter took Him aside and began to rebuke Him, saying, "God forbid it, Lord! This shall never happen to You." But He turned and said to Peter, "Get behind Me, Satan! You are a stumbling block to Me; for you are not setting your mind on God's interests, but man's." Then Jesus said to His disciples, "If anyone wishes to come after Me, let him deny himself, and take up his cross, and follow Me. For whoever wishes to save his life shall lose it; but whoever loses his life for My sake shall find it. For what will a man be profited, if he gains the whole world, and forfeits his soul? Or what will a man give in exchange for his soul?" (Matt. 16:21–26)

Shortly before His crucifixion, the disciples plied Jesus with questions concerning the end times.

And as He was sitting on the Mount of Olives, the disciples came to Him privately, saying, "Tell us, when will these things be, and what will be the sign of Your coming, and of the end of the age?" And Jesus answered and said to them, "See to it that no one misleads you. For many will come in My name, saying, 'I am the Christ,' and will mislead many. And you will be hearing of wars and rumors of wars; see that you are not frightened, for those things must take place, but that is not yet the end. For nation will rise against nation, and kingdom against kingdom, and in various places there will be famines and earthquakes. But all these things are merely the beginning of birth pangs." (24:3–8)

That same spirit of urgency and simplicity carried over to the apostles when they penned letters to the early church. Paul was no exception. He warned about the end times again and again.

Paul's Warnings

In both his letters to churches and to individuals, Paul raised the red flag whenever the subject turned to latter times.

But the Spirit explicitly says that in later times some will fall away from the faith, paying attention to deceitful spirits and doctrines of demons, by means of the hypocrisy of liars seared in their own conscience as with a branding iron, men who forbid marriage and advocate abstaining from foods, which God has created to be gratefully shared in by those who believe and know the truth. For everything created by God is good, and nothing is to be rejected, if it is received with gratitude; for it is sanctified by means of the word of God and prayer.

In pointing out these things to the brethren, you will be a good servant of Christ Jesus, constantly nourished on the words of the faith and of the sound doctrine which you have been following. (1 Tim. 4:1–6)[1]

Often during days of suffering we become even more intensely aware of the end (see 2 Tim. 2:1–15). In writing to his brothers and sisters in Christ who were suffering in the trenches of persecution, Peter himself intensifies his focus on the end times as he deploys the troops and briefs them for battle.

Marching Orders for Soldiers of the Cross

So far in his letter, Peter has been dealing with suffering saints, those who were being taken advantage of, and those who could not see relief in sight. Suddenly, he introduces the one thought that always brings a measure of relief: the end of all things. In doing so, he not only adds urgency to the moment, he simplifies the game plan. He leaves his readers with four commands to obey and one goal to pursue.

Four Commands to Obey

The first command is found in verse 7 of 1 Peter 4: *Use good judgment and stay calm in a spirit of prayer.*

The end of all things is at hand; therefore, be of sound judgment and sober spirit for the purpose of prayer.

Be of sound judgment. Be of sober spirit. Be calm. Don't be filled with anxiety. Don't quit your job. And don't think you have

1. See also 2 Timothy 3:1–5, Romans 14:10–12, and 1 Corinthians 4:5.

to know every detail of the end times in order to feel secure, as Warren Wiersbe rightly notes.

Early in my ministry, I gave a message on prophecy that sought to explain everything. I have since filed away that outline and will probably never look at it (except when I need to be humbled). A pastor friend who suffered through my message said to me after the service, "Brother, you must be on the planning committee for the return of Christ!" I got his point, but he made it even more pertinent when he said quietly, "I've moved from the program committee to the welcoming committee."

I am not suggesting that we not study prophecy, or that we become timid about sharing our interpretations. What I am suggesting is that we not allow ourselves to get out of balance because of an abuse of prophecy. There is a practical application to the prophetic Scriptures. Peter's emphasis on hope and the glory of God ought to encourage us to be faithful today in whatever work God has given us to do (see Luke 12:31–48).[2]

The secret of maintaining the balance and calmness that Wiersbe speaks about is prayer. That doesn't mean we dream our way into eternity. We are to pray and watch. In fact, prayer is what sharpens our awareness so that we'll be more discerning than we'd normally be. Prayer is what allowed Jesus to submit to His arrest, and the lack of it is what made Peter resist (compare Mark 14:32–42 with John 18:10–11).

The second command is: *Stay fervent in love for one another.*

Above all, keep fervent in your love for one another, because love covers a multitude of sins. (1 Pet. 4:8)

Fervent comes from the Greek word *ektenē*. Literally, it means "strained."[3] It's used of athletes straining to reach the tape or clear

2. Warren W. Wiersbe, *Be Hopeful* (Wheaton, Ill.: SP Publications, Victor Books, 1982), p. 107.

3. Edwin A. Blum, "1 Peter," *The Expositor's Bible Commentary*, ed. Frank E. Gaebelein (Grand Rapids, Mich.: Zondervan Publishing House, Regency Reference Library, 1981), vol. 12, p. 246.

the bar. The point is that if ever there's a time to stretch our love for one another to the limit, it's during the end times. And what is it that reveals this love? Forgiveness.

When Peter says that love covers a multitude of sins, he's alluding to the principle in Proverbs 10:12.

> Hatred stirs up strife,
> But love covers all transgressions.

3|15|06

Nothing is more disruptive to the unity of the body than Christians who are stirred up against one another and experiencing strife. And nothing is a poorer witness.[4] Mahatma Gandhi once said: "I like your Christ but I don't like your Christians . . . . They are so unlike your Christ."[5] And what is Christ like? He is characterized by forgiveness (Luke 7:48; Matt. 18:21–22; Luke 23:34). An insightful person once said, "We are most like beasts when we kill. We are most like men when we judge. We are most like God when we forgive."[6]

The third command Peter gives is: *Be hospitable toward one another.*

3|11|96

> Be hospitable to one another without complaint.
> (1 Pet. 4:9)

Underscore the words "one another." The same phrase is found in verses 8 and 10. It doesn't refer to just those who are lovable or friendly or fun to be with. It refers to all who are in the body of Christ, even the unlovely and unfriendly.

Another little phrase tacked on to the end of verse 9 is a crucial one when it comes to showing hospitality—"without complaint." What would bring about complaints? The trouble it takes to entertain people in your home. The expense. The time. But hospitality is never a problem when our priorities are in place, when love opens the door. Notice how verse 8 begins: "*Above all,* keep fervent in your love for one another."

But hospitality is not something we should abuse, which apparently

---

4. On the other hand, nothing is more of a compelling witness than the love and unity that Christians exhibit toward each other (John 13:34–35; 17:21). For more on this, consult Francis Schaeffer's books *The Mark of the Christian* and *The Church Before a Watching World.*

5. Quoted by Brennan Manning in *Lion and Lamb* (Old Tappan, N.J.: Fleming H. Revell Co., Chosen Books, 1986), p. 49.

6. *Quote/Unquote*, comp. Lloyd Cory (Wheaton, Ill.: SP Publications, Victor Books, 1977), p. 122.

was being done in the first century. And it was abused largely by people who were living unbalanced lives in response to prophetic teaching. They reasoned, "Since Christ is coming soon, why bother working, why not liquidate all assets and live off others?" Paul directly speaks to this heretical reasoning in 2 Thessalonians 3:6–15. Peter speaks to it more indirectly in the next two verses by promoting involvement in the local church and the exercise of our spiritual gifts. In fact, verses 10–11 contain his fourth command: *Keep serving one another.*

> As each one has received a special gift, employ it in serving one another, as good stewards of the manifold grace of God. Whoever speaks, let him speak, as it were, the utterances of God; whoever serves, let him do so as by the strength which God supplies. (1 Pet. 4:10–11a)

This is one of several sections in the New Testament on spiritual gifts—special abilities God has given the body of Christ with which to minister to one another until He returns.[7] Peter's point is that the gifts we have should be used in serving one another. That is how we become good stewards of our gifts (v. 10).

But note the warning in verse 11 that goes along with exercising our gifts. When we speak, it shouldn't be our own opinions and philosophies about life—it should be "the utterances of God." And when we serve, it shouldn't be in our own strength but "by the strength which God supplies."

A Goal to Pursue

The latter part of verse 11 ends with a purpose clause that reveals the logical reason we should obey these four commands.

> So that in all things God may be glorified through Jesus Christ, to whom belongs the glory and dominion forever and ever. Amen.

In everything, God gets the glory. How many church conflicts could be resolved if that were everybody's goal? How many egos would be put in their place if God's glory—not human glory—was at stake?

---

7. Other key passages are Romans 12:6–8, 1 Corinthians 12:28–30, and Ephesians 4:11–12.

When we keep His glory uppermost in our minds, it's amazing how much else falls into place. Since He gets the glory, we're more comfortable leaving the results with Him in His time. Since He gets the glory, our umbrella of love expands to cover others. Since He gets the glory, it's easier for us to show hospitality to others, for we're ultimately serving Him. Since He gets the glory, exercising our gifts is not a pain but a privilege.

Being motivated to seek God's glory in all things is a difficult assignment. One thing helps, however: Understanding that "the end of all things is at hand" (v. 7). If we understand that—truly understand that—Peter's four commands are easy to obey and his one goal a cinch to accomplish.

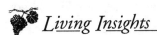 *Living Insights*_____ STUDY ONE

When we think about the end times, anxiety-ridden pictures elbow their way to the front of our minds. Pictures of people walking the sidewalks with placards that announce, The End Is Near! Pictures of people quitting their jobs and selling their possessions to camp on some communal mountaintop to wait for Christ's return. Pictures of preachers sensationalizing world events to alarm us into attending church.

But when we hear Peter preach about the end times, we are given a different set of pictures. Prudent pictures, tinted serenely with prayer. Family pictures, hued fervently with love. Hospitable pictures, without so much as a shadow of a complaint. Pictures that glow with the glory of God in every word spoken and in every service rendered.

What are some of the pictures that come to your mind when you think of the end times, and where did those pictures come from?

_____

_____

_____

_____

_____

_____

If you knew the end of all things was at hand and that you had only a short time—say, a month—how would you spend your time?

What one person would you want to share Christ with before the end came?

The words of Peter are as true today as they were two thousand years ago. The end is at hand. At any moment Jesus could return for His people. With sound judgment and sober spirit, won't you consider that as you pray for an opportunity to tell this person about the Savior?

Let's take a few minutes now to place the rough edges of our lives over the smooth edges of the Bible so we can trim off the selvage. In 1 Peter 4:7, Peter tells us to "be of sound judgment and sober spirit for the purpose of prayer." Place yourself up against the verse to see how well your life conforms to that command. On a one-to-ten scale, ten being complete compliance, how would you evaluate yourself?

1 2 3 4 5 6 7 8 9 10

What one thing could you do—or stop doing—that would move that a notch higher? (Cross references: 1 Peter 1:13; Philippians 4:4–7)

_____

_____

In 1 Peter 4:8, Peter encourages us to get our priorities straight: "Above all, keep fervent in your love for one another, because love covers a multitude of sins." How fervent is your love for those around you in the body of Christ?

1 2 3 4 5 6 7 8 9 10

What one thing could you do to move that a notch higher? (Cross references: 1 Peter 1:22; 1 John 4:20–21; 1 Corinthians 13:4–8)

_____

In 1 Peter 4:9, Peter instructs us to "be hospitable to one another without complaint." How would you rate yourself in this area?

1 2 3 4 5 6 7 8 9 10

When you show hospitality to others, what is it that sometimes turns you from a gracious host into a silently complaining house-keeper? (Cross references: Hebrews 13:2; Philippians 2:14)

_____

_____

In 1 Peter 4:10–11, Peter admonishes us to use our God-given gifts in serving one another. What is the special gift God has given you?

_____

How faithfully are you using that gift to serve others?

1   2   3   4   5   6   7   8   9   10

What could you do to be a better steward of that gift? (Cross references: 1 Corinthians 12:7, 12–27; Ephesians 4:11–16)

_____

_____

Peter concludes his paragraph about the end times by stating that the goal of all that we say and do should be the glory of God. How much of a motivation is that in your own life? (Cross references: Matthew 5:16; 1 Peter 2:12; 1 Corinthians 10:31)

_____

_____

Chapter 13

WHEN THROUGH FIERY TRIALS . . .

1 Peter 4:12–19

In his insightful book *The Problem of Pain*, C. S. Lewis said this about the role of trials in our lives.

> I am progressing along the path of life in my ordinary contentedly fallen and godless condition, absorbed in a merry meeting with my friends for the morrow or a bit of work that tickles my vanity to-day, a holiday or a new book, when suddenly a stab of abdominal pain that threatens serious disease, or a headline in the newspapers that threatens us all with destruction, sends this whole pack of cards tumbling down. At first I am overwhelmed, and all my little happinesses look like broken toys. Then, slowly and reluctantly, bit by bit, I try to bring myself into the frame of mind that I should be in at all times. I remind myself that all these toys were never intended to possess my heart, that my true good is in another world and my only real treasure is Christ. And perhaps, by God's grace, I succeed, and for a day or two become a creature consciously dependent on God and drawing its strength from the right sources. But the moment the threat is withdrawn, my whole nature leaps back to the toys.[1]

Such is human nature. And such is the nature of tribulations. Suffering under tribulations is the major theme of 1 Peter. The book is addressed to Christians who are going through desperate circumstances, many of which are undeserved, unfair, and unexpected. In today's lesson we want to take a closer look at the fiery trials through which we are sometimes called to walk. And we want to glean some practical insights to help us get through those times.

---

1. C. S. Lewis, *The Problem of Pain* (New York, N.Y.: Macmillan Co., 1962), p. 106.

Practical Truths about Trials

Before we delve into our text for today, let's turn to the book of James to get an overview about trials. James opens his book much the same way that Peter opens his. Peter writes to "scattered" Christians; James, to those who are "dispersed." Both recipients are strangers and aliens in a foreign land. To these strangers and aliens, James writes:

> Consider it all joy, my brethren, when you encounter various trials, knowing that the testing of your faith produces endurance. And let endurance have its perfect result, that you may be perfect and complete, lacking in nothing. (James 1:2–4)

From these three verses we learn a great deal about trials.

First: *Trials are common for Christians to encounter.* Notice that James says "when you encounter various trials"—not "if."

Second: *Trials come in various categories.* They may be physical, emotional, financial, relational, or spiritual. They may knock on the door of your business, your church, or your home. They may come at any time or at any season. They may be sudden, like a car accident, or prolonged, like a drawn-out court case. The trials may be public in nature or very private. They may be directly related to our own sin, the sin of others, or not related to sin at all.

Third: *Trials put our faith to the test.* No matter the source or the intensity, suffering drives us back to the basics, brings us back to the bedrock where our foundation rests.

Fourth: *Without trials, there could not be maturity.* James says we experience trials so that we may become "perfect and complete" (v. 4). The idea is of a plant that has matured to its maximum growth and fruitfulness.

Occasionally, trials are slight, brief, and soon forgotten. Other times, however, they linger and lean heavily upon us, leaving us exhausted and sometimes putting us on the sidelines. This latter category is what Peter is talking about when he writes of "the fiery ordeal."

Biblical Strength for Fiery Ordeals

In 1 Peter 4:12–19, Peter focuses in on this more intense form of suffering. The first two verses of that passage instruct us on *how to react.*

> Beloved, do not be surprised at the fiery ordeal

among you, which comes upon you for your testing, as though some strange thing were happening to you; but to the degree that you share the sufferings of Christ, keep on rejoicing; so that also at the revelation of His glory, you may rejoice with exultation. (vv. 12–13)

Interestingly, being surprised is usually our first response—"I can't believe this is happening." If, however, we view life as a schoolroom and God as the instructor, it should come as no surprise when we encounter pop quizzes and periodic examinations. Tests are not strange when we're involved in the pursuit of an educational degree. Neither are they strange when pursuing a curriculum of Christlikeness. Maturity in the Christian life is much like maturity in the classroom. It is measured by our ability to withstand the tests that come our way without having them shake our foundation or throw us into an emotional tailspin.

But our reaction should go beyond not being surprised (v. 12); it should include rejoicing. James puts it this way: "Consider it all joy . . ." (1:2). Why? Because trials enable us to enter into a closer partnership with Christ (Phil. 3:10) and because, if we endure them faithfully, we will receive a future reward (James 1:12).

Trials, therefore, become a means to a greater end: a deeper fellowship with Christ on earth and a richer reward from Him in heaven.

So much for how to react; now let's focus on *what to remember*. First: *Trials provide an opportunity to draw upon maximum power.*

If you are reviled for the name of Christ, you are blessed, because the Spirit of glory and of God rests upon you. (1 Pet. 4:14)

Remember that you are never closer, never more a recipient of His strength than when trials come upon you. This is especially true when we are reviled for the name of Christ (see also Matt. 5:10–12). The highest privilege is to suffer for the sake of Christ. At those times the Holy Spirit comes near and brings strength and a sense of God's glory. If you read the account of Stephen's martyrdom in Acts 7:54–60, that's exactly what happened to him.

The second thing to remember is: *Sometimes some of our suffering is deserved and shameful.*

By no means let any of you suffer as a murderer, or thief, or evildoer, or a troublesome meddler. (1 Pet. 4:15)

If the "fiery ordeal" comes as a result of our sinful behavior,[2] then we're not suffering for the glory of God but merely reaping the consequences of the seeds of wrongdoing we have sown (compare 1 Pet. 2:19–20; 3:17).

The third thing Peter wants us to remember is: *Most suffering should, in no way, cause us to feel shame.*

> But if anyone suffers as a Christian, let him not feel ashamed, but in that name let him glorify God. (4:16)

Instead of shame, we should feel honored when we suffer for our Lord. For it is a privilege to bear wounds for Him who was "pierced through for our transgressions" and "crushed for our iniquities" (Isa. 53:5). Such were the feelings of the apostles when they suffered for Christ.

> And they took his advice; and after calling the apostles in, they flogged them and ordered them to speak no more in the name of Jesus, and then released them. So they went on their way from the presence of the Council, rejoicing that they had been considered worthy to suffer shame for His name. (Acts 5:40–41)

The fourth thing Peter wants us to remember is: *Suffering is usually timely and needed.*

> For it is time for judgment to begin with the household of God. (1 Pet. 4:17a)

This is the most difficult thing to keep in mind, that we need to be purged, that the "house of God" needs not only daily dusting and sweeping but periodic "spring cleaning" as well. Remember this the next time a scandal surfaces in the church. Don't get disillusioned. It's just God refusing to let us sweep the dirt in His house under the rug.

The fifth thing Peter reminds us of in our passage for today is: *There is no comparison between what we suffer now and what the unrighteous will suffer later.*

---

2. It is interesting that the busybody or "troublesome meddler" is grouped in the same category with such reprehensible sinners as murderers, robbers, and evildoers. The term used for "troublesome meddler" literally means "one who oversees others' affairs."

If it begins with us first, what will be the outcome
for those who do not obey the gospel of God? And
if it is with difficulty that the righteous is saved,
what will become of the godless man and the sinner?
(vv. 17b–18)

If the righteous have "fiery ordeals" in their walk, imagine the
inferno that the lost will face in the future. Read Revelation
20:10–15 and take a few minutes to just imagine the horror.

So far in our passage Peter has told us how to react and what
to remember when going through fiery trials. Now he concludes his
discourse by telling us *on whom we are to rely.*

Therefore, let those also who suffer according to the
will of God entrust their souls to a faithful Creator
in doing what is right. (1 Pet. 4:19)

The key word in this verse is *entrust* (see also 1 Tim. 6:20; 2
Tim. 1:12, 14). It is a banking term and means "to deposit." "The
idea is that of depositing a treasure into safe and trustworthy
hands."[3] When it comes to trials, we deposit ourselves into God's
safekeeping. And that deposit yields eternal dividends.

The idea of entrusting our souls to God during trials can be
traced to Jesus' example on the cross, where He deposited His soul
into the care of His Father.

And Jesus, crying out with a loud voice, said, "Father, into Thy hands I commit[4] My spirit." And
having said this, He breathed His last. (Luke 23:46)

Personal Growth through All the Heat

The furnace of suffering provides not only light by which to
examine our lives but heat to melt away the dross. Just like the
famine and financial ruin of the prodigal son, trials are what bring
us to our senses and back to the Lord. The common response to
trials is one of resistance, if not outright resentment. But we should
open the door of our hearts and welcome them as honored guests
for the good they do in our lives.

3. R. C. H. Lenski, *The Interpretation of the Epistles of St. Peter, St. John and St. Jude* (Columbus,
Ohio: Wartburg Press, 1945), p. 213.

4. The word *commit* is the same Greek word that is translated "entrust" in 1 Peter 4:19.

Thus the terrible necessity of tribulation is only too clear. God has had me for but forty-eight hours and then only by dint of taking everything else away from me. Let Him but sheathe that sword for a moment and I behave like a puppy when the hated bath is over—I shake myself as dry as I can and race off to reacquire my comfortable dirtiness, if not in the nearest manure heap, at least in the nearest flower bed. And that is why tribulations cannot cease until God either sees us remade or sees that our remaking is now hopeless.[5]

As C. S. Lewis just noted, trials are not an elective in the Christian life; they are a required course. That course is a prerequisite to Christlikeness. But sometimes the tests are so gruelingly comprehensive that our tendency is to drop the course entirely. Especially if we feel abandoned by God.

If that's how you're feeling in the test you are going through now, you need to consult the course syllabus for a few guiding principles. First, when trials come, it's important to remember that God is faithful and that you can rely on Him. Second, when trials stay, it's important to remember to do the right thing and to take refuge in Him.

Living Insights STUDY ONE

In his book *Be Hopeful*, Warren Wiersbe has some insightful things to say about suffering.

"Suffering" and "glory" are twin truths that are woven into the fabric of Peter's letter. The world believes that the *absence* of suffering means glory, but a Christian's outlook is different. The trial of our faith today is the assurance of glory when Jesus returns (1 Pet. 1:7–8). This was the experience of our Lord (5:1), and it shall also be our experience.

But it is necessary to understand that God is not going to *replace* suffering with glory; rather He will *transform* suffering into glory.[6]

---

5. Lewis, *The Problem of Pain*, p. 107.

6. Warren W. Wiersbe, *Be Hopeful* (Wheaton, Ill.: SP Publications, Victor Books, 1982), pp. 115–16.

How is the pain of childbirth transformed into joy (see John 16:21)?

_____

_____

_____

How was Paul's thorn in the flesh transformed into power and glory (see 2 Cor. 12:7–10)?

_____

_____

_____

How was the shame and suffering of the Cross transformed into glory for the Lord Jesus (see Phil. 2:5–11)?

_____

_____

_____

How has suffering transformed your life? List specific ways in which you've suffered and the transforming effects the trials have produced.

Suffering: _____

Transforming effects: _____

_____

Suffering: _____

Transforming effects: _____

_____

Suffering: _____

Transforming effects: _____

_____

Some verses for further contemplation are Romans 5:3–5, 8:28–29, and 1 Peter 1:5–7.

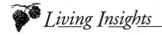

Reflect a few moments on this poignant analogy in Philip Yancey's book *Where Is God When It Hurts?*

Each of our individual deaths can be seen as a birth. Imagine what it would be like if you had had full consciousness as a fetus and could now remember those sensations:

Your world is dark, safe, secure. You are bathed in warm liquid, cushioned from shock. You do nothing for yourself; you are fed automatically, and a murmuring heartbeat assures you that someone larger than you fills all your needs. Your life consists of simple waiting—you're not sure what to wait for, but any change seems far away and scary. You meet no sharp objects, no pain, no threatening adventures. A fine existence.

One day you feel a tug. The walls are falling in on you. Those soft cushions are now pulsing and beating against you, crushing you downwards. Your body is bent double, your limbs twisted and wrenched. You're falling, upside down. For the first time in your life, you feel pain. You're in a sea of roiling matter. There is more pressure, almost too intense to bear. Your head is squeezed flat, and you are pushed harder, harder into a dark tunnel. Oh, the pain. Noise. More pressure.

You hurt all over. You hear a groaning sound and an awful sudden fear rushes in on you. It is happening—your world is collapsing. You're sure it's the end. You see a piercing, blinding light. Cold, rough hands pull at you. A painful slap. Waaaahhhhh!

Congratulations, you have just been born.

Death is like that. On this end of the birth canal, it seems fiercesome, portentous, and full of pain. Death is a scary tunnel and we are being sucked toward it by a powerful force.[7]

---

7. Philip Yancey, *Where Is God When It Hurts?* (Grand Rapids, Mich.: Zondervan Publishing House, 1977), p. 179.

The suffering we go through is also like that. It is a process of pulling some part of us through a birth canal, of delivering us from the cramped confines of a darkened womb to a world full of light and color and sound. Maybe that's what Jesus meant when He said that it was only in letting go of our lives that we truly learn to live. Is there some part of your life that is being pulled through a birth canal? Are you yielding to that tug or are you kicking to stay in the warm, soft security of the womb you're presently in? What is it you fear? What you will have to leave behind? The hand of Him who pulls you? The pain of the narrow canal through which you must travel? Or is it the uncertainty of what awaits you at the end of that journey?

Whatever it is, won't you take a breath between contractions and pray for the strength to go through this labor? Pray with the trust that He will be with you, holding your hand, and with the hope that your pain will soon be transformed into joy.

Chapter 14

JOB DESCRIPTION FOR SHEPHERDS

1 Peter 5:1–4

Charles Haddon Spurgeon was one of England's most noted preachers. At the age of twenty he was called to the pastorate at New Park Street Chapel in London. Soon after he took the pulpit, crowds swelled to overflowing capacity, necessitating the construction of the famous Metropolitan Tabernacle five years later in 1859. There Spurgeon preached until he retired on June 7, 1891. He died the following January. During his thirty-eight years as a pastor, he built a congregation of 6,000 and added more than 14,692 members to the church roster.

One biographer described this gifted man's contribution:

> Preeminently he was a preacher. His clear voice, his mastery of Anglo-Saxon, and his keen sense of humor, allied to a sure grasp of Scripture and a deep love for Christ, produced some of the noblest preaching of any age.[1]

Although he lived more than one hundred years ago (1834–1892), his prolific pen still pulsates with life, relevance, and wit. Some of Spurgeon's eloquence is preserved for us in his classic book *Lectures to My Students*. It is in this work that his pastoral heart beats the loudest. Listen to his words, and take note.

> Every workman knows the necessity of keeping his tools in a good state of repair. . . . If the workman lose the edge . . . he knows that there will be a greater draught upon his energies, or his work will be badly done. . . .
> . . . It will be in vain for me to stock my library, or organise societies, or project schemes, if I neglect the culture of myself; for books, and agencies, and

---

1. J. G. G. Norman, "Spurgeon, Charles Haddon," *The New International Dictionary of the Christian Church*, rev. ed., ed. J. D. Douglas (Grand Rapids, Mich.: Zondervan Publishing House, Regency Reference Library, 1978), p. 928.

systems, are only remotely the instruments of my holy calling; my own spirit, soul, and body, are my nearest machinery for sacred service; my spiritual faculties, and my inner life, are my battle axe and weapons of war.[2]

That same heart can be heard in the throb of Peter's words in our text for today, which deals with the right way to conduct one's ministry.

Practical Words of Exhortation regarding Expectations

Practically every ministry has one problem area that looms paramount, and that often has to do with expectations. This problem lies with the pastor as well as with his parishioners, because both begin their relationship with unrealistic expectations. The pastor expects a church with the commitment of the apostles, and the church, in turn, expects a pastor who can walk on water.

One of the secrets of long-term pastorates is clear-thinking realism, both on the part of the pastor and on the part of the congregation. Not every church can become a Metropolitan Tabernacle. And not every pastor can become a Charles Haddon Spurgeon.

In order to endure, pastors must be men who possess a great deal of patience, grace, understanding, and love. The same is true for congregations. Without such tolerance, few pastors would last thirteen months, let alone thirty-eight years, as Spurgeon did.

Biblical Guidelines for All Who Minister

Fortunately, the Bible shows us the way to foster tolerance and gives us some guidelines with which to form realistic expectations.

Two Effective Principles

Two effective principles regarding ministry shine forth like rays of light from the text of 1 Peter 5. The first is found in verse 1.

> Therefore, I exhort the elders among you, as your fellow elder and witness of the sufferings of Christ, and a partaker also of the glory that is to be revealed . . .

2. C. H. Spurgeon, *Lectures to My Students* (reprint, Grand Rapids, Mich.: Zondervan Publishing House, 1962), pp. 7–8.

First, *the pride of position must be absent.* It's easy for a pastor to become puffed up with his own importance. Why? Because he speaks for God. Because he stands in the spotlight. Because it's easy to live an unaccountable life. Because he's in control.

But that type of existence is like a private mine field, filled with buried dangers that could blow his ministry to smithereens with one careless step. Not even Peter, the Gibraltar among the disciples, considered himself invulnerable to the shrapnel of the pastorate. Look at the humility in his words—he appeals to the elders as a "fellow elder." The years have mellowed this old fisherman, for he doesn't view himself *above* them but *alongside* them; not apart from them but a *partner* with them.

The second illuminating principle is that *the heart of the shepherd must be present.*

> Shepherd the flock of God among you. (v. 2a)

The imperative "shepherd" finds its linguistic root in a Greek term that means "to act as a shepherd, to tend a flock." It is crucial to note that this flock is called "the flock of God." Technically speaking, they are not the pastor's people but God's people.[3] But still, the pastor should shepherd the flock with the same care God has for them. He should lead them into the green pastures of God's truth. He should seek them when they stray. He should protect them from predators. He should calm them in their fear and comfort them in their pain. Above all, the shepherd should love sheep. If he doesn't, he shouldn't apply for the pastorate.

Following these two effective principles are three all-important attitudes essential in bringing glory to God.

Three Essential Attitudes

Read the second half of verse 2 and all of verse 3 to see if you can spot these attitudes.

> Exercising oversight not under compulsion, but voluntarily, according to the will of God; and not for

---

3. "The comparison of God's people to a flock of sheep and the Lord to a shepherd is prominent in Scripture. (See, for example, Jacob's words: 'The God who has been my Shepherd all my life' [Gen. 48:15]; David's Shepherd Psalm [Ps. 23]; Ps. 100:3: 'We are His people, the sheep of His pasture'; Isa. 53:6–7; Luke 15:3–7, the parable of the lost sheep; and John 10:1–16.)" Edwin A. Blum, "1 Peter," *The Expositor's Bible Commentary,* ed. Frank E. Gaebelein (Grand Rapids, Mich.: Zondervan Publishing House, Regency Reference Library, 1981), p. 250.

sordid gain, but with eagerness; nor yet as lording it over those allotted to your charge, but proving to be examples to the flock.

First, an attitude of *willingness*—"not under compulsion, but voluntarily." The word *compulsion* means coercion or to be compelled by force.

One of the first things that characterizes burnout in the ministry is the lack of willingness. Often, that is brought on by depression. Spurgeon addressed this subject compassionately and realistically in his lectures.

Fits of depression come over most of us. Usually cheerful as we may be, we must at intervals be cast down. The strong are not always vigorous, the wise not always ready, the brave not always courageous, and the joyous not always happy. There may be here and there men of iron . . . but surely the rust frets even these.[4]

The second attitude is *eagerness*—"not for sordid gain, but with eagerness." The motivation for the ministry is not to be financial profit. The heart of the shepherd shouldn't be filled with a love for money but with a love for ministry. There should be an attitude of contagious zeal, not merely a willingness to serve but an effervescent enthusiasm that bubbles from the subterranean spring of the heart. Always remember that the ministry is a sacred position—not a profession to practice, but a debt to discharge.

The third attitude is *meekness*—"nor yet as lording it over . . . but proving to be examples." The idea of "lording it over" others is to exercise authority in such a way as to extend dominion over them, to think of them as underlings and yourself as boss.

But that is not the attitude Jesus had, and neither should we. We are not to think of ourselves as sovereign but as servants. We are fellow learners, sharers, partners, teammates.

The way we should exercise our influence is not as an authority but as an example. Our lives should be our sermons. The most inspiring leader is the one whose life speaks louder than his words.

4. C. H. Spurgeon, *Lectures to My Students*, (reprint, Grand Rapids, Mich.: Zondervan Publishing House, 1965), p. 154.

One Eternal Reward

So far we have looked at two effective principles and three essential attitudes. As we turn to verse 4, we want to conclude our study with one eternal reward.

> And when the Chief Shepherd appears, you will receive the unfading crown of glory. (v. 4)

For their exemplary service, these shepherds will receive an imperishable reward from the Good Shepherd himself (see 1 Cor. 3:10–14). But the reward is not doled out to everyone in the ministry. It's reserved for the faithful few who have fulfilled the job description in 1 Peter 5:1–3.

Personal Suggestions to Ministries Today

We want to footnote our study now with a few suggestions; first, to those who serve the Lord in leadership, and second, to all who are led.

To those who lead: *Keep a healthy balance.* If you teach, remain a good student. Read, listen, learn, observe, and most importantly, change. Since you are called to lead, follow well. Remember that there are few more powerful tools than a servant's spirit. When you lead, put yourself in your followers' shoes. Try to stay objective. Neither underestimate nor exaggerate your role. Recognize that though you are called by God, you can't do it all. Delegate, and when you do, don't forget to delegate the credit for the job as well. Though your work is serious, don't forget your sense of humor. Though admonition is a part of your job, don't forget to balance it with affirmation. And remember: sheep must be led, not driven. Finally, work hard, but know when to say when; you don't want to wind up as a workaholic, now do you.

To those who are led: *Be a reason for rejoicing.*

Here are a few suggestions for being a joy to those who lead: Think of ways to encourage your leader. Model gratitude and love. Defend the leader whenever possible. Try to imagine being in his shoes. And think of how it would be if all the others being led were just like you—would it be a drudgery or a delight?

Finally, hang Hebrews 13:7 over your heart.

> Remember those who led you, who spoke the word of God to you; and considering the result of their conduct, imitate their faith.

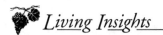 *Living Insights*

Peter tells us that the shepherd of God's flock is to lead by example (1 Pet. 5:3). But whose example does the shepherd follow? That of the Chief Shepherd himself (v. 4).

Read John 10:1–18. List several qualities of a "good shepherd" that we see exemplified in Christ.

_____

_____

_____

_____

_____

_____

Now turn to that age-old favorite, Psalm 23, where the metaphor of a shepherd is applied to God the Father. List several qualities of a good shepherd that we see exemplified in God's relationship to His people.

_____

_____

_____

_____

_____

Of those qualities you listed from the two passages, which one is the most incarnate in your life?

_____

Which is the least?

_____

For additional study in this area, pick up a copy of Phillip

Keller's excellent book *A Shepherd Looks at Psalm 23* and a copy of *A Shepherd Looks at the Good Shepherd and His Sheep.*

Living Insights

For those in leadership positions, it is essential to learn to keep a healthy balance in all areas of your life. Stop a minute, and ask yourself, "How balanced am I?" The following self-test should answer that question.

Am I a good student as well as a good teacher? □ Yes □ No □ So-so

Am I a good listener? □ Yes □ No □ So-so

Am I growing? □ Yes □ No □ So-so

Do I have a servant's spirit? □ Yes □ No □ So-so

Am I objective? □ Yes □ No □ So-so

Do I have a balanced view of my role? □ Yes □ No □ So-so

Do I delegate responsibility? □ Yes □ No □ So-so

Do I have a sense of humor? □ Yes □ No □ So-so

Do I balance admonition with affirmation? □ Yes □ No □ So-so

Do I balance my work with my other responsibilities (to God, to my family, to myself) □ Yes □ No □ So-so

For those who are led, it is essential to be a reason for rejoicing. Are you? This questionnaire should reveal whether you are or not.

Do you think of ways to encourage your leader? □ Yes □ No □ So-so

Do you model gratitude and love? □ Yes □ No □ So-so

Do you defend your leader whenever possible? □ Yes □ No □ So-so

Do you imagine being in the leader's shoes? □ Yes □ No □ So-so

Would you want to lead someone like yourself? □ Yes □ No □ So-so

For further study in this area of pastoral ministry, we've listed several good books that you will want for your library.

Anderson, Robert C. *The Effective Pastor*. Chicago, Ill.: Moody Press, 1985.

Engstrom, Ted W. *The Making of a Christian Leader*. Grand Rapids, Mich.: Zondervan Publishing House, 1976.

Hendricks, Howard G. *Teaching to Change Lives*. Portland, Oreg.: Multnomah Press and Walk Thru the Bible Ministries, 1987.

Hughes, Kent and Barbara. *Liberating Ministry from the Success Syndrome*. Wheaton, Ill.: Tyndale House Publishers, 1987.

Peterson, Eugene H. *Five Smooth Stones for Pastoral Work*. Atlanta, Ga.: John Knox Press, 1980.

Richards, Lawrence O., and Clyde Hoeldtke. *Church Leadership: Following the Example of Jesus Christ*. Grand Rapids, Mich.: Zondervan Publishing House, Ministry Resources Library, 1980.

White, John. *Excellence in Leadership*. Downers Grove, Ill.: Inter-Varsity Press, 1986.

Wiersbe, Warren W., and David Wiersbe. *Making Sense of the Ministry*. 1983. Reprint. Grand Rapids, Mich.: Baker Book House, 1989.

Chapter 15

A FORMULA
THAT BRINGS RELIEF
1 Peter 5:5–7

O ur society has gorged itself on the sweet taste of success. We've filled our plates from a buffet of books that range from dressing for success to investing for success. We've passed the newsstands and piled our plates higher with *Gentleman's Quarterly, Vogue,* or *The Wall Street Journal.* And when we've devoured these, we have turned our ravenous appetites toward success-oriented seminars. We've gobbled down whole notebooks and cassette albums in our hunger for success.

The irony of it all is that

> there is never enough success in anybody's life to make one feel completely satisfied.[1]

Instead of fulfillment, we experience the bloated sensation of being full of ourselves, *our* dreams, *our* goals, *our* plans, *our* projects. The result of that all-you-can-eat appetite is not contentment— it's nausea.

If you find yourself a little queasy after a steady diet like that, you don't need a second helping of success; you need to learn how to be satisfied. That's where 1 Peter 5:5–7 comes in.

Today's Major Messages, Promising "Success"

The ad campaigns that come out of Madison Avenue promise much more than they can really deliver. These titillating messages fall into four categories.

The first is *fortune.* The subliminal message is that to be successful, you need to make a great deal of money. Although money is not sinful or suspect in itself, it is not what brings either happiness or fulfillment.

The second is *fame.* To be successful, they say, you need to become known in the public arena. You need to be a celebrity, a

---

1. Jean Rosenbaum, quoted in *Quote/Unquote,* comp. Lloyd Cory (Wheaton, Ill.: SP Publications, Victor Books, 1977), p. 315.

social somebody. In this view, fame and popularity become the twin sisters of significance.

The third is *power*. To be successful, some say, you need to wield a lot of authority, flex your muscle, take charge, be in control, carry a lot of weight.

The fourth is *pleasure*. To be successful, the messages imply, you need to be able to do whatever feels good. This philosophy operates on the pleasure principle, "If it feels good, do it." But it's not a modern philosophy at all; it's really just the ancient epicurean philosophy of "eat, drink, and be merry."

Take a step back from these four messages that bombard us from the billboards. Fortune. Fame. Power. Pleasure. What's missing? A vertical dimension. There's not even a hint of God's will or what pleases Him. Note also that there is nothing in that list which will guarantee satisfaction or bring relief deep within the heart.

God's Ancient Plan, Bringing Relief

Contrary to the world's formulas for success, God's formula does offer relief.

> You younger men, likewise, be subject to your elders; and all of you, clothe yourselves with humility toward one another, for God is opposed to the proud, but gives grace to the humble.
> Humble yourselves, therefore, under the mighty hand of God, that He may exalt you at the proper time, casting all your anxiety upon Him, because He cares for you. (1 Pet. 5:5–7)

The world's strategy to climb the ladder of success is simple: Work hard, get ahead, don't let anything get in your way, and promote yourself. The goal is to make it to the top. It doesn't matter who you step on along the way. And it doesn't matter who you leave behind, even if it's your family or your friends. It's a dog-eat-dog world, they tell you, and the puppies don't make it. To survive, you have to hold on to the ladder for dear life. To succeed, you have to claw your way to the top.

Peter, however, has a different strategy for success. In fact, in those three verses there is a series of contrasts to that kind of thinking. The first has to do with *authority*. We are to submit ourselves to those who are wise and to "clothe" ourselves with humility (v. 5).

120

The metaphor Peter uses comes from a rare word which pictures a servant putting on an apron before serving those in the house. Perhaps Peter is recalling that last meal in the Upper Room where Jesus girded Himself with a towel and washed the disciples' feet (John 13:4–17).

The imperative to "be subject to" is in the present tense. Submission is to be an ongoing way of life. We are to listen to the counsel of the elders, be open to their reproofs, watch their lives and follow the examples they set, accept their decisions, and respect their years of seasoned wisdom.

Why? Because to do otherwise leads to proud independence. This results in a backlash of consequences, the main one being the opposition of God (see also James 4:6). The idea of God opposing the proud is found in Proverbs 3.

> Do not envy a man of violence,
> And do not choose any of his ways.
> For the crooked man is an abomination to the
>   Lord;
> But He is intimate with the upright.
> The curse of the Lord is on the house of the
>   wicked,
> But He blesses the dwelling of the righteous.
> Though He scoffs at the scoffers,
> Yet He gives grace to the afflicted.
> The wise will inherit honor,
> But fools display dishonor.
> (vv. 31–35)

In contrast to the humble, those who are proud in their hearts *scoff* at the Lord. The term is an expression of scorn, derision, or contempt. But God, not the proud, has the last scoff! As Solomon puts it, "He scoffs at the scoffers."

The second strategy Peter suggests for success has to do with *attitude.* There is no more important attitude for success than this: to humble ourselves under God's mighty hand (1 Pet. 5:6).

In the Old Testament, God's hand symbolizes two things. The first is discipline (see Exod. 3:20; Job 30:21; Ps. 32:4). The second is deliverance (Deut. 9:26; Ezek. 20:34). When we humble ourselves under the mighty hand of God, we willingly accept His discipline as being for our good and for His glory. And we gratefully acknowledge His deliverance that is always in His time and in His way.

121

In other words, we don't manipulate people or events. And we don't hurry His timing. We let Him set the pace. The result of this attitude? "He may exalt you at the proper time" (1 Pet. 5:7). (See also Phil. 2:5–9; James 4:10.)

David serves as a good illustration of this attitude. As a young musician, he didn't go on tour trying to make a name for himself: he sang to his sheep. He continued to write his lyrics without thought of being published. He eventually became known as a skillful musician whom the Lord was with (1 Sam. 16:18). As a result of David's staying close to God and submitting to Him, God exalted the lowly shepherd to the highest position in the land— as shepherd of the entire nation (Ps. 78:70–72).

Peter's third strategy for success has to do with *anxiety*. We are to cast all our anxiety upon Him. The original meaning of the term *cast* literally is translated "to throw upon." It represents a decisive action on our part that is neither passive nor partial. We might translate the term to read, "Heave it over." When those anxieties that accompany growth and true success begin to weigh you down, heave them upon the Lord.

> Cast your burden upon the Lord, and He will
> sustain you;
> He will never allow the righteous to be shaken.
> (Ps. 55:22)

Want a simple formula that will enable you to not only handle whatever success God may bring your way but provide you with the relief you need? Here it is:

SUBMISSION + HUMILITY – WORRY = RELIEF

Submission to others plus humility before God minus the worry of the world equals genuine relief!

Our Great Need, Effecting Change

In order for us to get a grasp of what true success really is and how to obtain it, we need to tune out the seductive messages from the world and tune in to the instructive messages from the Word. Our great need is a three-dimensional one.

We need *direction* so we can know to whom we should submit.

We need *discipline* to restrain our hellish pride.

We need *discernment* so we can spot the beginning of anxiety.

And how are those needs met? Through the Word of God, which gives us direction (Ps. 119:105), discipline (2 Tim. 3:16), and discernment (Ps. 119:98–100).

Do you find yourself caught up in the success syndrome? Are you still convinced that the world's formula is the best? Do you find yourself manipulating people and pulling strings to obtain success? That type of success never satisfies. Only God's success offers the formula that brings real relief.

🍇 Living Insights

Pick up a magazine or newspaper that you have around the house. Leaf through the pages, and pay particular attention to the advertisements. Read between the lines, looking for any subliminal messages for success in each of the four categories we reviewed in our lesson. Then jot them down below.

Fortune_____

_____

_____

_____

Fame_____

_____

_____

_____

Power_____

_____

_____

_____

Pleasure_____

_____

_____

_____

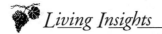 *Living Insights*

Look up the following verses to see what God has to say about fortune, fame, power, and pleasure.

Fortune

Proverbs 23:4–5 _____

_____

Matthew 6:19–21 _____

_____

1 Timothy 6:9–10 _____

_____

Fame

Isaiah 40:6–8 _____

_____

Jeremiah 9:23–24 _____

_____

1 John 2:15–17 _____

_____

Power

Deuteronomy 8:17–18 _____

_____

Psalm 62:11 _____

_____

2 Corinthians 3:5; 4:7 _____

_____

Pleasure

1 Timothy 4:3–5 _____

_____

Ecclesiastes 2:1–11 _____

_____

Ecclesiastes 2:24–25 _____

_____

Chapter 16

STANDING NOSE-TO-NOSE
WITH THE ADVERSARY

1 Peter 5:8–11

First Peter was written to people in pain. Interestingly, Peter doesn't lament over that fact, nor does he offer his advice on how to escape it. Instead, he faces it squarely, tells us not to be surprised by it, and even says that God provides benefits for enduring suffering. So, even when life is dreary and overcast, there are rays of hope that pierce through the clouds to stimulate our growth. In fact, without some pain there would be little growth at all, for we would remain sheltered, delicate, naive, and immature.

The tendency when suffering rains down upon us is to think that God has withdrawn His umbrella of protection and abandoned us. But Peter suggests just the opposite. He says that there is every reason to hope and to be encouraged because even in suffering God is there and at work in our lives.

Our confusion during those inclement times stems from our lack of understanding about the role of pain in our lives.

> Christians don't really know how to interpret pain. If you pinned them against the wall, in a dark, secret moment, many Christians would probably admit that pain was God's one mistake. He really should have worked a little harder and invented a better way of coping with the world's dangers.[1]

The ultimate culprit for so much of the world's pain and danger is our adversary the devil. Although God is at work in the trials of lives, so is Satan. While God uses the trial to draw us closer to Him, Satan uses it as a lever to pry us away from Him.

In our lesson for today Peter gives us some crucial advice on how to do battle with the devil and keep him from gaining victory over our lives.

---

1. Philip Yancey, *Where Is God When It Hurts?* (Grand Rapids, Mich.: Zondervan Publishing House, 1977), pp. 22–23.

A Quick Overview of 1 Peter 5

Before we delve into our passage for today, let's take a step back to gain an overview of 1 Peter 5. As we survey the chapter, five things stand out. First, overall it's a chapter of wise commands and advice. Second, the initial advice is to elders on shepherding the flock (vv. 1–4). Third, the advice to the rest of us is on being successful (vv. 5–7). Fourth, the last piece of advice deals with Satan (vv. 8–11). Fifth, Peter closes the chapter with some personal comments (vv. 12–14).

In our section for today, verses 8–11, Peter reaches a crescendo in his passion. In our last section he exhorted us to humility; in this section he exhorts us to resistance. In our last section he called us to cast our anxieties upon God; in this section he calls us to take up arms against our adversary.

Sober Instructions on Battle Tactics

In his book *Your Adversary the Devil*, Dwight Pentecost compares the tactics of a physical battle to those of the spiritual one.

> No military commander could expect to be victorious in battle unless he understood his enemy. Should he prepare for an attack by land and ignore the possibility that the enemy might approach by air or by sea, he would open the way to defeat. Or should he prepare for a land and sea attack and ignore the possibility of an attack through the air, he would certainly jeopardize the campaign.
>
> No individual can be victorious against the adversary of our souls unless he understands that adversary; unless he understands his philosophy, his methods of operation, his methods of temptation.[2]

His Identity and Style

First Peter 5:8 sheds some valuable insight on understanding our adversary.

Be of sober spirit, be on the alert. Your adversary,

---

2. J. Dwight Pentecost, *Your Adversary the Devil* (Grand Rapids, Mich.: Zondervan Publishing House, 1969), Introduction.

the devil, prowls about like a roaring lion, seeking someone to devour.

The term *adversary* refers to an opponent in a lawsuit.[3] The other term used to describe our adversary is *the devil*, which means "slanderer" or "accuser."[4] In Revelation 12:10 he is referred to as the "accuser of our brethren." Every fiber of his being is bent on defaming and defeating us.

The way he does this is by stealth. He "prowls about," stalking our every step, waiting for a strategic moment to take us off guard. He pads about "like a roaring lion," ravenous with hunger. His goal? To devour us.

Our Response and Reason

As prey, our primary response should be to keep on the lookout for the predator.

> Satan is a dangerous enemy. He is a serpent who can bite us when we least expect it. He is a destroyer (Rev. 12:11; "Abaddon" and "Apollyon" both mean "destruction") and an accuser (Rev. 12:9–11; Zech. 3:1–5). He has great power and intelligence, and a host of demons who assist him in his attacks against God's people (Eph. 6:10ff). He is a formidable enemy; we must never joke about him, ignore him, or underestimate his ability. We must "be sober" and have our minds under control when it comes to our conflict with Satan.[5]

The devil's great hope is to be ignored, written off as a childhood fairy tale, and dismissed from the mind of the educated adult. Just like a prowler breaking into a home, Satan doesn't want to call attention to himself. He wants to work incognito in the shadows. The thing he fears most is a flashlight turned in his direction, revealing who he really is and what he is really up to.

3. The Greek term is *antidikos*. See also Job 1:6–19 and Zechariah 3:1.

4. The Greek term is *diabolos*. "According to Scripture, he has great power on earth, 'being the prince of this world' (John 14:30) and 'the ruler of the kingdom of the air' (Eph. 2:2). But God has limited his activity. Through his captive subjects (Eph. 2:2, 2 Tim. 2:25–26), the devil attempted to destroy the infant church by persecution." Edwin A. Blum, "1 Peter," *The Expositor's Bible Commentary*, ed. Frank E. Gaebelein (Grand Rapids, Mich.: Zondervan Publishing House, Regency Reference Library, 1981), vol. 12, p. 252.

5. Warren W. Wiersbe, *Be Hopeful* (Wheaton, Ill.: SP Publications, Victor Books, 1982), p. 138.

To defeat the devil we must first respect—not fear or revere—but respect him, like an electrician respects the power of electricity. The second thing we must do is resist him, as Peter exhorts in verse 9.

> But resist him, firm in your faith, knowing that the same experiences of suffering are being accomplished by your brethren who are in the world. (1 Pet. 5:9)

Kenneth Wuest comments on this verse.

> The Greek word translated "resist" means "to withstand, to be firm against someone else's onset" rather than "to strive against that one." The Christian would do well to remember that he cannot fight the devil. The latter was originally the most powerful and wise angel God created. He still retains much of that power and wisdom as a glance down the pages of history and a look about one today will easily show. While the Christian cannot take the offensive against Satan, yet he can stand his ground in the face of his attacks. Cowardice never wins against Satan, only courage.[6]

Once we have enough respect for Satan's insidious ways to stay alert and ready for his attacks, the best method for handling him is strong resistance. That resistance is not in our own strength but comes from being "firm *in faith*." An example of such resistance can be seen in the wilderness temptations of Christ when He resisted Satan with the Word of God (Matt. 4:1–11).

Here is where Christians have the jump on all others who do battle with this cunning adversary. Although our strength is insufficient to successfully fend him off, when we draw on the limitless resources of faith, we can stand against him nose-to-nose. And that faith is nurtured and strengthened by a steady intake of the Scriptures (see Rom. 10:17; Ps. 119:9, 11).

In addition to the strength that comes from such faith, there is also a company of saints stretching down through history, as well as present-day believers, joining hands across the globe. There is something wonderfully comforting about knowing that we are not alone in the battle against the adversary (see Heb. 12:1–3).

6. Kenneth S. Wuest, *First Peter: In the Greek New Testament* (Grand Rapids, Mich.: William B. Eerdmans Publishing Co., 1956), p. 130.

Pain and Rewards

In spite of faith and in spite of friends in the faith, battle with the archenemy is excruciating. It requires strength that is not our own and a steadfast faith that digs in and refuses to relinquish even an inch of ground. But the good news is this: when resisted this way, he will retreat (James 4:7). And that is the subject of the next verse.

> And after you have suffered for a little while, the God of all grace, who called you to His eternal glory in Christ, will Himself perfect, confirm, strengthen and establish you. (1 Pet. 5:10)

Will there be suffering in resisting Satan? Yes. Will it be painful? Without a doubt. We might even emerge from the battle a little shell-shocked. But after the dust settles, there are rewards, medals of honor that our Commander in chief will pin on our lapels—He will "perfect" us, "confirm" us, "strengthen" us, and "establish" us.

Verse 10 is the picture of a decorated war hero, a seasoned veteran whose muscles of faith have been hardened by battle. It is the portrait of the well-grounded, stable, mature Christian.

Christ will make sure the portrait of our lives looks like that, for He Himself will hold the brush. And His hand is vastly more powerful than our enemy's, for, as verse 11 tells us,

> to Him be dominion forever and ever. Amen.

He is the one who has "the dominion." And He has it "forever and ever." He is the one *ultimately* in control. And that is something in which every believer can find hope.

A Couple of Necessary Reminders

To remember what we've studied today, we want to tie a couple of strings around your finger. One is to remind you of something never to do. The other is to remind you of something to always do.

First: *Never* confuse confidence in Christ with cockiness in the flesh.

Second: *Always* remember that suffering is temporal and its rewards are eternal.

> Therefore we do not lose heart, but though our outer man is decaying, yet our inner man is being renewed day by day. For momentary, light affliction is

producing for us an eternal weight of glory far beyond all comparison, while we look not at the things which are seen, but at the things which are not seen; for the things which are seen are temporal, but the things which are not seen are eternal. (2 Cor. 4:16–18)

Our Lord set the example for us, "who for the joy set before Him endured the cross" (Heb. 12:2). We have all read the Gospel accounts that chronicle Christ's suffering on the cross. We have all heard the Good Friday sermons that recount the horrors of crucifixion. As we look up at Him there on the cross, we can all sense His shame and feel the anguish of His heart as we stand at arm's length from His torn and feverish flesh.

What we can't see is the joy that awaited Him when He surrendered His spirit to His Father. But He saw it. He knew. Imagine for a minute how horrible was the nightmare of the Cross. Then imagine, if you can, how wonderful the joy awaiting Jesus must have been for Him to have willingly endured that degree of suffering and injustice. That same joy awaits us. But we have to stoop through the low archway of suffering to enter into it.

🍇 *Living Insights* STUDY ONE

If Satan is a subject you've always avoided, it's time you searched the Scriptures to find out who he is and how he works. Dwight Pentecost, in his book *Your Adversary the Devil*, tells us why this is essential.

> If we are going to be victorious in the warfare into which we were thrust the moment we accepted Jesus Christ as Saviour, we need to understand that large body of Scripture that reveals to us the person and the work of the one with whom we are at war. It is our desire to examine the Scriptures to learn from their extensive revelation the nature of our adversary, the Devil, his devices, deceits, doctrines, designs—so that we may detect his movements in our daily experience. Victory may be ours. But victory depends on knowledge.[7]

7. Pentecost, *Your Adversary the Devil*, Introduction.

Below is a list of Pentecost's chapter titles and the main Scripture references that he covers in his book. Reading through the passages will give you a good overview of this all-important subject.

The Fall of Satan	Ezekiel 28:11–19
The Sin of Satan	Isaiah 14:12–17
The Hierarchy of Satan	Ephesians 6:10–17
Satan's Conquest of the Earth	Genesis 3:1–7
Satan, the Deceiver	1 Timothy 4:1–8
Satan, the Perverter	Isaiah 5:18–23
Satan, the Imitator	2 Corinthians 11:1–15
Satan, the Lawless One	2 Thessalonians 2:1–12
Satan, the Rebel	Job 1:6–2:7
Pursued by a Roaring Lion	1 Peter 5:8–9
The Doctrine of Satan	2 Peter 1:16–2:22
Satan's Response to the Preaching of the Word	Matthew 13:1–22
How Satan Tempts	Matthew 4:1–11
Satan's Steps in Temptation	1 John 2:15–17, see also James 1:13–16
How Satan Operates	Matthew 17:14–21
Christ's Conquest of Satan	Colossians 2:9–15
The Believer's Authority Over Satan	Ephesians 2:1–10
Putting the Adversary to Flight	James 4:1–8
Trafficking with Demons	Deuteronomy 18:9–13
Satan's Destiny	Revelation 20:1–10

 *Living Insights* STUDY TWO

There is probably no book as insightful concerning the strategies of Satan than C. S. Lewis' book *The Screwtape Letters*. In the preface he warns:

> There are two equal and opposite errors into which our race can fall about the devils. One is to disbelieve in their existence. The other is to believe, and to feel an excessive and unhealthy interest in them.[8]

8. C. S. Lewis, *The Screwtape Letters* (New York, N.Y.: Macmillan Publishing Co., 1961), p. 3.

Below is a sampling of Satan's strategy as articulated by Screwtape, a senior devil, who corresponds with his eager nephew to educate the fledgling devil for warfare against the forces of "the Enemy" (i.e., God).

> Like all young tempters, you are anxious to be able to report spectacular wickedness. But do remember, the only thing that matters is the extent to which you separate the man from the Enemy. It does not matter how small the sins are, provided that their cumulative effect is to edge the man away from the Light and out into the Nothing. Murder is no better than cards if cards can do the trick. Indeed, the safest road to Hell is the gradual one—the gentle slope, soft underfoot, without sudden turnings, without milestones, without signposts.[9]

To assist you in becoming more alert to the subtle strategies of our adversary and to resist his cunning attacks, we heartily recommend that you pick up a copy of *The Screwtape Letters*. It is a great book for either personal reflection or group discussion.

1 15min

2 Listen Journel.

3 Prayer
Proverb —

9. Lewis, *The Screwtape Letters*, p. 56.

Chapter 17

REFLECTIONS SEEN
IN PETER'S INK
1 Peter 1–5

J ust as the reflections of parents can be seen in the lives of their
children, so the reflections of writers can be seen in their letters.
First Peter is no exception. In it we see the apostle's zeal, his courage,
his humility, his tenderness, and his forthrightness. The words in the
letter fit together like mosaic tiles, revealing a composite of the big
fisherman upon whose rocklike leadership the church at Jerusalem
was founded.

But there are other reflections in the letter besides a picture of
the author. Today we want to step back and review what those
reflections are. As we do, we'll notice five general observations,
three major messages, and four lasting lessons.

Five General Observations

As we look at this letter from a distance, a few broad-stroked
observations immediately stand out in sharp relief.

First: *Peter wrote the letter.* Though this may seem obvious, this
fact offers us a unique encouragement. Along with James and John,
Peter was one of the inner circle of confidants to whom Jesus
revealed Himself most fully (Matt. 17:1–13; 26:36–46). Of the
twelve disciples, Peter was regarded as the spokesman (Matt.
16:13–16; Acts 2:14–40). Never one to teeter on the fence of
indecision, Peter was impulsive, impetuous, and outspoken (Matt.
14:28–29; John 18:10; Matt. 17:4). He knew the heights of ecstasy
on the Mount of Transfiguration (Matt. 17:1–13) and the depths
of misery on the night of his denial (Matt. 26:69–75). And yet, in
spite of his flaws and his failures, he is called an apostle (1 Pet. 1:1a).

This is tremendous encouragement for all who fear that their
flaws are too numerous or their failures too enormous to be given
a second chance.

Second: *Hurting people received the letter.* They are not named,
but their locations are stated in verse 1.

> To those who reside as aliens, scattered throughout
> Pontus, Galatia, Cappadocia, Asia, and Bithynia. (v. 1b)

These hurting people, scattered outside their homeland, were lonely, frightened, and unsure of their future. But though they were aliens, they were not abandoned; though they were frightened, they were not forgotten.

> Who are chosen according to the foreknowledge of
> God the Father, by the sanctifying work of the Spirit,
> that you may obey Jesus Christ and be sprinkled with
> His blood: May grace and peace be yours in fullest
> measure. (vv. 1b–2)

Whenever you find yourself in a strange place away from home where you feel like an alien, 1 Peter is great reading. It will assure you of your calling and reassure you that grace and peace can be yours to claim "in fullest measure."

Third: *This letter came through Silas.* The one to whom Peter dictated his words was Silas, one of the leaders in the early church, although he is referred to in 1 Peter 5:12 as Silvanus.[1]

> Through Silvanus, our faithful brother (for so I
> regard him), I have written to you briefly, exhorting
> and testifying that this is the true grace of God.
> Stand firm in it!

Peter was a rugged fisherman, a blue-collar Galilean with little or no schooling. Silas, however, was a cultured Roman citizen, well educated and well traveled. Apparently, beginning with 5:12, Peter actually took the pen in his own hand and wrote the final lines. We know that, not only because of the substance of verses 12–14, but because of the style. The grammar, syntax, and vocabulary become immediately simple in the original Greek.

Fourth: *The letter concludes with a greeting from a woman.*

> She who is in Babylon, chosen together with you,
> sends you greetings, and so does my son, Mark. (v.13)

This cryptic ending begs the question: who is this woman Peter

---

1. See Acts 15:22–33, 15:40–18:5; 1 Thessalonians 1:1; 2 Thessalonians 1:1. For a full discussion on the equating of Silvanus with Silas, see Edward Gordon Selwyn's commentary *The First Epistle of St. Peter*, 2d ed. (1947; reprint, London, England: Macmillan Press, 1974), pp. 9–17.

refs to? The interpretation falls into two categories: Peter could either be referring to "woman" in the figurative sense, as the bride of Christ, or he could be using the word literally. If the latter category is the correct interpretation, the woman referred to is very possibly Peter's own wife.[2]

Fifth: *The letter's final command is one of intimate affection.*

> Greet one another with a kiss of love. Peace be to you all who are in Christ. (v. 14)

The formal kiss was the sign of peace among early Christians, demonstrating their love and unity (see 1 Cor. 16:20). This outward kiss reflected an inward peace between believers, a sign that all injuries were forgiven and forgotten.[3]

So much for the bookends that open and close Peter's letter. Now let's take a last look at the contents. In reading through the letter, you've probably found three places where Peter specifically addresses his readers with major messages.

Three Major Messages

Peter mentions his readers in 1:1–2, 2:11, and finally in 4:12. These direct addresses give us a clue to the epistle's structure. The letter falls neatly into three distinct sections, each one detailing the "how" of an important truth: a living hope and how to claim it (1:1–2:10), a pilgrim life and how to live it (2:11–4:11), a fiery trial and how to endure it (4:12–5:11).

A Living Hope and How to Claim It

We first find the message of the "living hope" in 1:3.

> Blessed be the God and Father of our Lord Jesus Christ, who according to His great mercy has caused us to be born again to a living hope through the resurrection of Jesus Christ from the dead.

2. See Mark 1:30. In 1 Corinthians 9:5, Paul makes note of the other apostles' wives, which likely included Peter's wife. Clement of Alexandria states that she died as a martyr for the faith, so she may have been well-known to the early Christians when Paul wrote his letter.

3. This is what made Judas' kiss all the more deceitful. "Judas' choice of the kiss to enable his company to identify Jesus points to its having been in frequent use between Jesus and His disciples. By the middle of the second century it was in regular use in the liturgy at the conclusion of the prayers and immediately before the offertory." Selwyn, *The First Epistle of St. Peter,* p. 244.

If you read carefully, you'll find this idea occupying Peter's mind all the way through 2:10. And how do we claim that living hope? By focusing on the Lord (1:2, 7, 11, 13, 18–20), and by trusting in His Word (1:23–2:2).

The Pilgrim Life and How to Live It

As Christians, we live in a world that is not our home; we live as pilgrims on a journey to another land. How do we live this pilgrim life? By submission—in the realm of government (2:13–17), in the realm of occupation (vv. 18–20), in the realm of home (3:1–7), and in the realm of the church (vv. 8–12). For ultimately, we are not submitting to human authority but to divine authority (2:13–14).

The Fiery Trial and How to Endure It

No matter how fiery the trial, it's important to remember that the temperature is ultimately regulated by God's sovereignty (4:12–19). And it's also important to understand that we don't suffer our trials in isolation; we are part of a flock that is lovingly tended by faithful shepherds (5:1–5). Finally, we need to know that no matter how formidable our adversary, the power of God is available to help us endure (vv. 6–11).

And how do we endure the fiery trials that engulf us? By cooperation. We need to cooperate with God by trusting Him (4:19), with the leadership of the church by submitting to them (5:5), and with faith by standing firm and resisting the onslaught of the devil (5:9).

Four Lasting Lessons

Through these five general observations and three major messages, the ink from Peter's pen has made an indelible impression on our lives. But beyond these are four lasting lessons, four secrets of life, that stand out in bold letters.

First: *When our faith is weak, joy strengthens us.* Let's look at two passages in 1 Peter which underscore that lesson.

> In this you greatly rejoice, even though now for a little while, if necessary, you have been distressed by various trials, that the proof of your faith, being more precious than gold which is perishable, even though tested by fire, may be found to result in praise and glory and honor at the revelation of Jesus Christ; and though you have not seen Him, you love Him,

137

and though you do not see Him now, but believe in Him, you greatly rejoice with joy inexpressible and full of glory. (1:6–8)

> Beloved, do not be surprised at the fiery ordeal among you, which comes upon you for your testing, as though some strange thing were happening to you; but to the degree that you share the sufferings of Christ, keep on rejoicing; so that also at the revelation of His glory, you may rejoice with exultation. (4:12–13)

No matter how dark the clouds, the sun will eventually pierce the darkness and dispel it; no matter how heavy the rain, the sun will ultimately prevail to hang rainbows in the sky. So joy will chase away the clouds hanging over our faith and prevail over the disheartening trials that drench our lives (see also Ps. 30:5; John 16:20–22).

Second: *When our good is mistreated, endurance stabilizes us.* Remember the words of 1 Peter 2:19–20?

> For this finds favor, if for the sake of conscience toward God a man bears up under sorrows when suffering unjustly. For what credit is there if, when you sin and are harshly treated, you endure it with patience? But if when you do what is right and suffer for it you patiently endure it, this finds favor with God.

The word *endure* in verse 20 means "to bear up under a load," as a donkey bears up under the load its owner has placed on its back. This patient bearing of life's cumbersome loads is made possible by love (1 Cor. 13:7), made steadfast by hope (1 Thess. 1:3), and made easier by example (2 Tim. 3:10–11).

Third: *When our confidence is shaken, love supports us.* Love is the pillar of support when our world comes crumbling down around us. That's why, when warning about the end times, Peter puts love on the top of the survival checklist.

> Above all, keep fervent in your love for one another, because love covers a multitude of sins. (1 Pet. 4:8)

Fourth: *When our adversary attacks, resistance shields us.* When Satan stalks us like a roaring lion, we're not instructed to freeze, to hide, or to tuck tail and run; we're told to resist. And that resistance forms a shield to protect us from his predatory claws.

Be of sober spirit, be on the alert. Your adversary, the devil, prowls about like a roaring lion, seeking someone to devour. But resist him, firm in your faith, knowing that the same experiences of suffering are being accomplished by your brethren who are in the world. (5:8–9)

As we reach the end of our study in Peter's first letter, it's really not important how many of his words we have been through; what's important is how much his words have been through us. Because, you see, it's not how well we grasp Peter's words that will make a difference in our lives; it's how Peter's words grasp us.

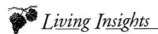 *Living Insights*

Let's take a closer look at the three major messages of 1 Peter.

A Living Hope and How to Claim It

Why is the hope in 1 Peter 1:3 referred to as "living"?

_____

What would that hope be like if Jesus hadn't been raised from the dead (see 1 Cor. 15:17–19)?

_____

How does the resurrection of Christ have future application for the believer (see 1 Cor. 15:20–28)?

_____

_____

_____

How does it have present application (see Rom. 6:4–14)?

_____

_____

_____

A Pilgrim Life and How to Live It

If our true home is heaven, how should that affect us as we live our lives here on earth?

Matthew 6:19–21 _____

_____

_____

Philippians 3:20_____

_____

_____

Colossians 3:1–2 _____

_____

_____

A Fiery Trial and How to Endure It

What happens to metal under stress if it hasn't been sufficiently heat-treated?

_____

_____

Why, then, are fiery trials necessary?

_____

_____

_____

How is endurance developed in our lives (see Rom. 5:3; James 1:3)?

_____

What is the benefit of enduring trials (see Rom. 5:3–5; James 1:4)?

_____

_____

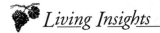 *Living Insights*

Now let's turn our attention from Peter's three major messages to his four lasting lessons.

When Our Faith Is Weak, *Joy* Strengthens Us

Look up the following Scriptures on joy: 2 Corinthians 7:4; Colossians 1:24; Hebrews 12:2; James 1:2.

What do these verses have in common? _____

What is the Lord saying to you through these verses? _____

_____

_____

When Our Good Is Mistreated, *Endurance* Stabilizes Us

What are some reasons why endurance is so important?

Hebrews 12:1 and Jeremiah 12:5 _____

_____

Hebrews 12:5–11 _____

_____

James 5:11 _____

_____

According to Isaiah 40:28–31, what great promise does God give to those lacking endurance?

_____

_____

When Our Confidence Is Shaken, *Love* Supports Us

How is God's love for us a support when things are shaky (see Rom. 8:31–39)?

_____

_____

How is our love for God a support when circumstances undermine our confidence (see Rom. 8:28)?

_____

_____

From 1 Peter 4:8–9, what is a tangible way we can show our love to other Christians?

_____

_____

From Hebrews 13:1–3, what are some other ways (see also Matt. 25:34–40)?

_____

_____

_____

_____

When Our Adversary Attacks, *Resistance* Shields Us

What is the assurance we have if we resist the devil (see James 4:7)?

_____

What principle about resistance do we learn from Ecclesiastes 4:12?

_____

_____

What is essential if we are to successfully resist the forces of the enemy (see Eph. 6:13–17)?

_____

_____

Chapter 18

Unraveling the Mystery
of Suffering
2 Corinthians 1:1–11

Running through the fabric of 1 Peter like a muted thread is the theme of suffering. Intertwined with that theme is the finely spun truth that suffering should be a cause for rejoicing.

Like a choir master, Peter has instructed us not only to rejoice but to "rejoice with exultation" (1 Pet. 4:13). Trying to be obedient to Peter's instruction, the stately, robed choir sings with one accord:

> Come, ye disconsolate, where'er ye languish;
> Come to the Mercyseat, fervently kneel.
> Here bring your wounded hearts, here tell your
>   anguish;
> Earth has no sorrow that Heav'n cannot heal.[1]

But despite the angelic harmony of the choir and the fervent desire to follow Peter's counsel, a discordant note plucks at the heartstrings of many in the pews who suffer. Their pain may be physical, marital, financial, or emotional . . . afflicting a friend, a relative, an immediate family member, or themselves. Whatever the circumstances, those who suffer carry in their hearts a tangle of emotions, entwined with all kinds of questions, both personal and theological: "Why? Why *this*? Why *me*? Why *now*?"

Peter has given us practical advice as to how we should respond to suffering, but we need to turn to Paul to discover the *why*—to unravel the mystery of suffering. Hopefully, this study in 2 Corinthians will nimble up your mental fingers so you can sort out all the winding threads that may have tied your life in painful knots.

Peter has given us practical advice

This lesson has been adapted from chapter 2 of "Unraveling the Mystery of Suffering," from the study guide A Ministry Anyone Could Trust, coauthored by Ken Gire, from the Bible-teaching ministry of Charles R. Swindoll (Fullerton, Calif.: Insight for Living, 1989), pp. 12–20.

1. Thomas Moore, "Come, Ye Disconsolate," The Lutheran Hymnal (St. Louis, Mo.: Concordia Publishing House, 1941), no. 531.

Suffering: Understanding Its Reality

One thing knits us all together into the same tapestry—suffering. Its throbbing threads are woven throughout our lives: death, divorce, bankruptcy, cancer, heart disease, scandal, kidnapping, rape. From our earthly perspective, all we see are twisted knots. No wonder we look up, straining to see some design, some purposeful pattern, and ask why.

Suffering: Unraveling Its Mystery

The Bible gives us a glimpse of the heavenward side of that tapestry in the first eleven verses of 2 Corinthians. This passage faces the mystery of suffering head-on and begins to untangle it strand by strand.

Warm Words of Introduction

Written by a man whose authority had often been undermined, 2 Corinthians begins by verifying Paul's credentials.

> Paul, an apostle of Christ Jesus by the will of God, and Timothy our brother, to the church of God which is at Corinth with all the saints who are throughout Achaia. (1:1)

Paul calls himself "an apostle of Christ Jesus." The word *apostolos* literally means "one sent forth." It was used to describe that unique first-century individual who was gifted with the miraculous ability to speak as an oracle of God. There were only twelve apostles in the technical sense of the word—Jesus' original eleven disciples plus Judas' replacement.

Paul was an apostle not because he inherited the role, not because he was selected by the people or appointed by some commission, and not because he appointed himself. He was an apostle "by the will of God." In contrast, Paul describes Timothy affectionately as a *brother*. The young pastor is not an apostle but rather an apostolic delegate.

The letter is addressed to the church at Corinth and was meant to be forwarded from that commercial center to the concentric circle of believers radiating throughout the region of Achaia.[2]

---

2. Achaia was the Roman province comprising all the territory of Greece south of Macedonia. Presumably, copies of the letter would be made at Corinth and then circulated throughout the province.

With the formalities aside, Paul greets them warmly.

Grace to you and peace from God our Father and
the Lord Jesus Christ. (v. 2)

Grace is a key word for Paul. It is God doing for us that which
we don't deserve and cannot repay. And in its wake comes peace.
Peace is a freedom from inner distraction, an inner rest. Grace and
peace don't come from ourselves—no matter how positive our
thoughts; or from others—no matter how assuring their counsel.
They come only from God.

Wise Words of Explanation

Since so much of his letter focuses on pain, suffering, and heartache, it's not surprising that Paul explains some of the reasons
behind these trials.

Blessed be the God and Father of our Lord Jesus
Christ, the Father of mercies and God of all comfort;
who comforts us in all our affliction so that we may
be able to comfort those who are in any affliction
with the comfort with which we ourselves are comforted by God. (vv. 3–4)

The word *comfort* almost leaps off the page and is central to
Paul's explanation. In verses 3–7, the same root word is used ten
times. It comes from the Greek word *paraklētos*, which is formed
from the prefix *para*, meaning "alongside," and the root *kaleō*, meaning "to call." Comfort is given by someone called alongside to
help—like a nurse called to a patient's bedside. The word is also
used as another name for the Holy Spirit in John 14:16—"And I
will ask the Father, and He will give you another Helper [Com-
forter], that He may be with you forever."

When tragedy strikes, collapsing our life like a house of cards,
that's when we cry out to God. That's when we need comfort. That's
when we need someone to come alongside and put an arm around
us, to be there, to listen, to help. Though God is often silent during
those times, He's always there . . . as the *Paraklētos*, the Father of
mercies and the God of all comfort.

In explaining why we suffer, Paul lists three reasons in verses
4–11. The first is found in verse 4.

Who comforts us in all our affliction so that we may

be able to comfort those who are in any affliction with the comfort with which we ourselves are comforted by God.

First: *That we might be prepared to comfort others.* It's like a chain reaction: when we go through suffering, God comforts us. And when His comfort has done its work in our lives, then we, in turn, can comfort others. A perfect example of this is Joni Eareckson Tada. God has comforted her in her affliction, and she, in turn, has comforted thousands of other people who also have physical disabilities. The person who has suffered the shattering effects of a divorce can best comfort a divorcée. The person who has lost a child can best comfort another parent whose baby has died. The businessman who once was bankrupt can best comfort another person in the throes of financial disaster. So one reason God allows suffering is that we might have a well of experiences deep enough to draw the compassion and counsel we need to comfort others.

Some of us may worry that we won't have enough comfort to offer those who are writhing in an anguished valley of pain. But Paul relieves this concern in verse 5.

> For just as the sufferings of Christ are ours in abundance, so also our comfort is abundant through Christ.

God's salve is dispensed in proportion to the extent of our wounds. And that salve is stored in us so at the appropriate time we might dispense it to others.

> But if we are afflicted, it is for your comfort and salvation; or if we are comforted, it is for your comfort, which is effective in the patient enduring of the same sufferings which we also suffer; and our hope for you is firmly grounded, knowing that as you are sharers of our sufferings, so also you are sharers of our comfort. (vv. 6–7)

Lest we think Paul's advice is only theoretical, he shares a dark chapter from his life to show us that these principles come straight from the textbook of real life.

> For we do not want you to be unaware, brethren, of our affliction which came to us in Asia, that we were burdened excessively, beyond our strength, so that

we despaired even of life; indeed, we had the sentence
of death within ourselves. (vv. 8–9a)

Whatever his affliction in Asia, it was more than he could bear,
and it pushed him to the brink of death's abyss.[3] While teetering
on that brink, though, Paul discovered a second reason for suffering.

Indeed, we had the sentence of death within ourselves in order that we should not trust in ourselves,
but in God who raises the dead. (v. 9)

Second: *That we might not trust in ourselves*. Intense suffering is
designed to remind us of our utter helplessness. For it is when we
are most helpless that we are most dependent. Since our understanding is finite and feeble, we should acknowledge that handicap
and seek the support which is infinitely stronger.

Trust in the Lord with all your heart,
And do not lean on your own understanding.
In all your ways acknowledge Him,
And He will make your paths straight.
(Prov. 3:5–6)

The reason we don't depend on God more is because we all too
often follow the world's wisdom, which is diametrically opposed to
the wisdom of Proverbs. We have been indoctrinated by a pull-
yourself-up-by-your-own-bootstraps philosophy. In a country whose
most prized document is the Declaration of Independence, it's easy
to see why we have such a hard time leaning, trusting, and depend-
ing on God.

Turning to another highly prized document, we come to the
book of Jeremiah. Through the impassioned pen of the weeping
prophet—himself well-acquainted with grief—God gives one of
the grandest promises in all the Bible.

"'For I know the plans that I have for you,' declares
the Lord, 'plans for welfare and not for calamity to
give you a future and a hope.'" (29:11)

---

3. With his back against the wall, Paul sees himself wedged in a crushing situation from
which there is no escape. "The rare word *exaporethenai* ('despaired') implies the total un-
availability of an exit." Murray J. Harris, "2 Corinthians," *The Expositor's Bible Commentary*,
ed. Frank E. Gaebelein (Grand Rapids, Mich.: Zondervan Publishing House, Regency Reference Library, 1976), vol. 10, p. 321.

Signed, "God." Isn't that a tremendous love note? This word from God will help you endure your present suffering, enabling you to look beyond your painful circumstances and see the outcome, the future, the hope. You may think there's no rhyme or reason to the doggerel verse of pain you're experiencing. But in God's eyes, your pain is just the first draft of a poem in the making.

Paul concludes this section of his letter with a thank-you note that provides the third reason why we suffer.

> Who delivered us from so great a peril of death, and will deliver us, He on whom we have set our hope. And He will yet deliver us, you also joining in help-ing us through your prayers, that thanks may be given by many persons on our behalf for the favor bestowed upon us through the prayers of many. (2 Cor. 1:10–11)

Third: *That we might learn to give thanks in everything.* Not until we can say "Thank You, Lord," have we fully accepted suffering's yoke. A whole new dimension of the tapestry comes into view when we learn to shoulder the yoke with thanksgiving (compare Lam. 3:27–32 with 1 Thess. 5:18).

But this doesn't mean we take the tragic things in our lives and overlay them with a gold-leaf veneer, parroting praise as a form of denial. Not at all. God doesn't want us to give thanks *for* everything but, rather, *in* everything. Just because by God's grace "All things work together for good" for the one who loves God, it doesn't mean that all things that happen to us *are* good in and of themselves (Rom. 8:28).

Suffering: Handling Its Perplexities

> That we might be prepared to comfort others.
> That we might not trust in ourselves.
> That we might learn to give thanks in everything.

Almost sounds like a stanza out of an old hymn, doesn't it? Suffering *can* be transformed into a song. Here are three suggestions to turn your discordant notes of pain into beautiful music.

One, instead of focusing only on yourself now, think of how you can help others later. This will sound a note of hope. Two, rather than fighting, surrender; rather than resisting, release. This will produce a note of faith. And three, although in the case of suffering inflicted by others, getting even seems to come more naturally, try giving thanks instead. This will bring a note of peace. Hope. Faith. Peace. Hear the melody? Hear the harmony? Let Christ turn your suffering into a symphony. And where there was only the whining of instruments warming up, let Him orchestrate a musical score that would make even Mozart stand up and applaud.

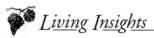 *Living Insights*

It's easy to wax eloquent on the benefits of suffering when your life is relatively pain-free. But finding good in heartache is much more difficult when you are in the midst of it. Hurting people were the audience Peter addressed. And, most probably, his letter has had your name on the envelope too.

If you finished his letter and still couldn't make sense of the suffering you're going through, maybe Paul's words in 2 Corinthians have helped. As you review the first eleven verses of 2 Corinthians 1, use the space that follows to record half-a-dozen key words. These words should stand out to you due to their significance to the overall text. See if you can define each word from the context. If you can't, consult a Bible dictionary. Finally, write a statement as to why you think the word is significant.

2 Corinthians 1:1–11

Key word:_____

Definition: _____

_____

Significance: _____

_____

Key word:_____

Definition: _____

_____

Significance: _____

_____

Key word:_____

Definition: _____

_____

Significance: _____

_____

Key word:_____
Definition: _____

_____

Significance: _____

_____

Key word:_____
Definition: _____

_____

Significance: _____

_____

Key word:_____
Definition: _____

_____

Significance: _____

_____

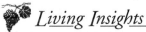 *Living Insights* _____

Like Peter, the apostle Paul was no stranger to suffering, and he brings out some helpful strategies for coping in a time of crisis. These strategies are well worth reviewing. If you're going through a tough time right now, write down ways to apply these three statements or tell how these principles helped you through a past crisis.

1. Instead of focusing only on yourself now, think of how you can help others later.

_____

_____

_____

_____

_____

_____

_____

2. Rather than fighting, surrender; rather than resisting, release.

_____

_____

_____

_____

_____

_____

3. Although in the case of suffering inflicted by others, getting even seems to come more naturally, try giving thanks instead.

_____

_____

_____

_____

_____

_____

BOOKS FOR
PROBING FURTHER

Thornton Wilder's novel *The Eighth Day* concludes philosophically with this analogy.

> History is *one* tapestry. No eye can venture to compass more than a hand's-breadth. . . .
> There is much talk of a design in the arras. Some are certain they see it. Some see what they have been told to see. Some remember that they saw it once but have lost it. Some are strengthened by seeing a pattern wherein the oppressed and exploited of the earth are gradually emerging from their bondage. Some find strength in the conviction that there is nothing to see. Some[1]

He ends the novel there, with an incomplete thought, expecting his readers to finish the sentence for themselves.

How would *you* finish it?

Peter would finish by saying that it's God working behind the tapestry, weaving together the variegated threads of our lives to serve His pattern. Some of those threads are bright; others, muted; still others, black. Peter would tell us that we can delight even in the threads of suffering interwoven through our lives—delight not in the darkness of the threads themselves, but in how they enhance the pattern of God's tapestry.

Admittedly, the divine pattern is not so easy to see when the shuttle of suffering passes through the warp and woof of our own lives. It takes perspective to see what is woven, as well as patience with the weaver as He slowly wends the dark threads through our lives. To help give you the perspective you need—and the patience —we have provided the following books for your reference.

---

1. Thornton Wilder, *The Eighth Day* (New York, N.Y.: Harper and Row, Publishers, 1967), p. 435.

Commentaries on 1 Peter

Blum, Edwin A. "1 Peter." *The Expositor's Bible Commentary.* Volume 12. Ed. Frank E. Gaebelein. Grand Rapids, Mich.: Zondervan Publishing House, Regency Reference Library, 1981. This modern work combines grammatical insights, historical background, and practical exegesis to provide a balanced treatment of 1 Peter. Although the Greek is consulted regularly, the book is accessible for the layperson as well as the student.

Clowney, Edmund. *The Message of 1 Peter.* The Bible Speaks Today series. Downers Grove, Ill.: InterVarsity Press, 1988. Well-written and thorough, this student's commentary is meant more to be read than simply referred to. The author not only provides insightful historical background but also relates Peter's words to our world today.

Selwyn, Edward Gordon. *The First Epistle of St. Peter.* 2d ed. London, England: Macmillan Press, 1947. This commentary on the Greek text is a classic work for the serious student. In addition to scholarly exegesis, the author provides a number of enlightening word studies, insightful essays, and additional notes.

When You Are Suffering

Biebel, David B. *If God Is So Good, Why Do I Hurt So Bad?* Colorado Springs, Colo.: NavPress, 1989. The author provides an understanding look at the journey from pain to wholeness. The aim is pastoral and the tone is personal, for much of what Biebel has written comes from his own painful experiences as a father who lost his firstborn son.

Books for Those Who Hurt. Fullerton, Calif.: Insight for Living, 1989. This booklet, compiled by our counseling staff at Insight for Living, contains information about dozens of books that can provide specific help for the particular issues you are struggling with today. To obtain this index, just write to us—our address is listed on the order form at the back of this study guide.

Foxe, John. *Foxe's Book of Martyrs.* Reprint. Ed. W. Grinton Berry. Grand Rapids, Mich.: Baker Book House, 1987. This volume was written in the sixteenth century and remains a classic today. It recounts the suffering and martyrdom of Christians throughout history, from the first century to the time of the author's death.

Lewis, C. S. *The Problem of Pain.* New York, N.Y.: Macmillan Publishing Co., Collier Books, 1962. This stimulating, deeply reflective treatise on suffering runs the gamut of difficult questions—from divine goodness to human wickedness, from human pain to animal pain, from heaven to hell. Lewis was professor of Medieval and Renaissance literature at Cambridge University and was, quite possibly, the greatest intellectual gift to Christianity in the twentieth century.

Martin, James. *Suffering Man, Loving God.* San Francisco, Calif.: Harper and Row, Publishers, 1990. Offering intelligent, empathetic insights into the issue of suffering, this book shows how Jesus' example teaches us to help others who are suffering, keep faith in the midst of trial, and transform suffering prayerfully.

Schaeffer, Edith. *Affliction.* Old Tappan, N.J.: Fleming H. Revell Co., Power Books, 1978. With her personal and vivid style of writing, the author combs through Scripture and her own experience to help the reader understand the role of affliction in the life of the believer.

Yancey, Philip. *Where Is God When It Hurts?* Grand Rapids, Mich.: Zondervan Publishing House, 1977. Winner of the Gold Medallion Award for excellence in Christian publishing, this book is probably the best single volume to address the tough questions when it comes to pain and suffering.

When You Are Under Attack

Lewis, C. S. *The Screwtape Letters.* Revised paperback edition. New York, N.Y.: Macmillan Publishing Co., 1982. As we learned in our study of Peter's first letter, Satan is the ultimate culprit behind much of the world's suffering. In this, one of Lewis' most profound and intriguing books, the author exposes some of our enemy's more subtle strategies and opens our eyes to ways we can resist him.

Some of these books may be out of print and available only through a library. For those currently available, please contact your local Christian bookstore. Books by Charles R. Swindoll may be obtained through Insight for Living. IFL also offers some books by other authors—please note the ordering information that follows and contact the office that serves you.

ORDERING INFORMATION

HOPE IN HURTFUL TIMES
Cassette Tapes and Study Guide

This Bible study guide was designed to be used independently or in conjunction with the broadcast of Chuck Swindoll's taped messages which are listed below. If you would like to order cassette tapes or further copies of this study guide, please see the information given below and the order forms provided at the end of this guide.

		U.S.	Canada
HHT	Study guide	$ 4.95 ea.	$ 6.50 ea.
HHTCS	Cassette series, includes all individual tapes, album cover, and one complimentary study guide	59.50	69.50
HHT 1–9	Individual cassettes, includes messages A and B	6.00 ea.	7.48 ea.

The prices are subject to change without notice.

HHT 1-A: *Peter: The Man and His Message*—Survey of 1 Peter
     B: *How We Can Smile through Suffering*—1 Peter 1:1–12

HHT 2-A: *Staying Clean in a Corrupt Society*—1 Peter 1:13–21
     B: *Reasons for Pulling Together*—1 Peter 1:22–2:3

HHT 3-A: *Several Portraits of Solid Saints*—1 Peter 2:4–12
     B: *Pressing On Even Though Ripped Off*—1 Peter 2:13–25

HHT 4-A: *The Give-and-Take of Domestic Harmony*—1 Peter 3:1–7
     B: *Maturity Checkpoints*—1 Peter 3:8–12

HHT 5-A: *When Life "Just Ain't Fair"*—1 Peter 3:13–17
     B: *Crucifixion, Proclamation, Resurrection, Exaltation*— 1 Peter 3:18–22

HHT 6-A: *How to Shock the Pagan Crowd*—1 Peter 4:1–6
     B: *Four Commands . . . One Goal*—1 Peter 4:7–11

HHT 7-A: *When through Fiery Trials . . .*—1 Peter 4:12–19
     B: *Job Description for Shepherds*—1 Peter 5:1–4

HHT 8-A: *A Formula That Brings Relief*—1 Peter 5:5–7
     B: *Standing Nose-to-Nose with the Adversary*—1 Peter 5:8–11

HHT 9-A: *Reflections Seen in Peter's Ink*—1 Peter 1–5
B: *Unraveling the Mystery of Suffering*—
2 Corinthians 1:1–11

How to Order by Phone or FAX
(Credit card orders only)

United States: 1-800-772-8888 from 7:00 A.M. to 4:30 P.M., Pacific time, Monday through Friday
FAX (714) 575-5496 anytime, day or night

Canada: 1-800-663-7639, Vancouver residents call (604) 532-7172 from 8:00 A.M. to 5:00 P.M., Pacific time, Monday through Friday
FAX (604) 532-7173 anytime, day or night

Australia and the South Pacific: (03) 9-872-4606 or FAX (03) 9-874-8890 from 8:00 A.M. to 5:00 P.M., Monday through Friday

---

Other International Locations: call the Ordering Services Department in the United States at (714) 575-5000 during the hours listed above.

How to Order by Mail

United States
• Mail to: Processing Services Department
Insight for Living
Post Office Box 69000
Anaheim, CA 92817-0900
• Sales tax: California residents add 7.25%.
• Shipping and handling charges must be added to each order. See chart on order form for amount.
• Payment: personal checks, money orders, credit cards (Visa, Master-Card, Discover Card, and American Express). No invoices or COD orders available.
• $10 fee for *any* returned check.

Canada
• Mail to: Insight for Living Ministries
Post Office Box 2510
Vancouver, BC V6B 3W7
• Sales tax: please add 7% GST. British Columbia residents also add 7% sales tax (on tapes or cassette series).
• Shipping and handling charges must be added to each order. See chart

156

on order form for amount.
- Payment: personal cheques, money orders, credit cards (Visa, Master-Card). No invoices or COD orders available.
- Delivery: approximately four weeks.

Australia and the South Pacific
- Mail to: Insight for Living, Inc.
  GPO Box 2823 EE
  Melbourne, Victoria 3001, Australia
- Shipping: add 25% to the total order.
- Delivery: approximately four to six weeks.
- Payment: personal checks payable in Australian funds, international money orders, or credit cards (Visa, MasterCard, and BankCard).

Other International Locations
- Mail to: Processing Services Department
  Insight for Living
  Post Office Box 69000
  Anaheim, CA 92817-0900
- Shipping and delivery time: please see chart that follows.
- Payment: personal checks payable in U.S. funds, international money orders, or credit cards (Visa, MasterCard, and American Express).

Type of Shipping	Postage Cost	Delivery
Surface	10% of total order*	6 to 10 weeks
Airmail	25% of total order*	under 6 weeks

*Use U.S. price as a base.

Our Guarantee
Your complete satisfaction is our top priority here at Insight for Living. If you're not completely satisfied with anything you order, please return it for full credit, a refund, or a replacement, as you prefer.

Insight for Living Catalog
The Insight for Living catalog features study guides, tapes, and books by a variety of Christian authors. To obtain a free copy, call us at the numbers listed above.

Order Form
United States, Australia, and Other International Locations
(Canadian residents please use order form on reverse side.)

HHTCS represents the entire *Hope in Hurtful Times* series in a special album cover, while HHT 1–9 are the individual tapes included in the series. HHT represents this study guide, should you desire to order additional copies.

HHT	Study guide	**$ 4.95 ea.**
HHTCS	Cassette series,	**59.50**
	includes all individual tapes, album cover, and one complimentary study guide	
HHT 1–9	Individual cassettes,	**6.00 ea.**
	includes messages A and B	

Product Code	Product Description	Quantity	Unit Price	Total
			$	$

Amount of Order	First Class	UPS
$ 7.50 and under	1.00	4.00
$ 7.51 to 12.50	1.50	4.25
$12.51 to 25.00	3.50	4.50
$25.01 to 35.00	4.50	4.75
$35.01 to 60.00	5.50	5.25
$60.00 and over	6.50	5.75

Fed Ex and Fourth Class are also available. Please call for details.

If you are placing an order after January 1, 1997, please call for current prices.

Prices are subject to change without notice.

Order Total	
UPS ❑ First Class ❑ *Shipping and handling must be added. See chart for charges.*	
Subtotal	
California Residents—Sales Tax Add 7.25% of subtotal.	
Non-United States Residents *Australia add 25%. All other locations: U.S. price plus 10% surface postage or 25% airmail.*	
Gift to Insight for Living *Tax-deductible in the United States.*	
Total Amount Due *Please do not send cash.*	$

Payment by: ❑ Check or money order payable to Insight for Living   ❑ Credit card

(Circle one):   Visa   MasterCard   Discover Card   American Express   BankCard _(In Australia)_

Number _____

Expiration Date _____   Signature _____

We cannot process your credit card purchase without your signature.

Name _____

Address _____

City _____   State _____

Zip Code _____   Country _____

Telephone (_____) _____   Radio Station ____ ____ ____ ____

If questions arise concerning your order, we may need to contact you.

Mail this order form to the Processing Services Department at one of these addresses:

Insight for Living
Post Office Box 69000, Anaheim, CA 92817-0900

Insight for Living, Inc.
GPO Box 2823 EE, Melbourne, VIC 3001, Australia

Order Form
Canadian Residents

(Residents of the United States, Australia, and other international locations, please use order form on reverse side.)

HHTCS represents the entire *Hope in Hurtful Times* series in a special album cover, while HHT 1–9 are the individual tapes included in the series. HHT represents this study guide, should you desire to order additional copies.

HHT	Study guide	$ 6.50 ea.
HHTCS	Cassette series,	69.50
	includes all individual tapes, album cover, and one complimentary study guide	
HHT 1–9	Individual cassettes, includes messages A and B	7.48 ea.

Product Code	Product Description	Quantity	Unit Price	Total
			$	$

Amount of Order	Canada Post		
Orders to $10.00	2.00	**Subtotal**	
$10.01 to 30.00	3.50	**Add 7% GST**	
$30.01 to 50.00	5.00	**British Columbia Residents** Add 7% sales tax on individual tapes or cassette series.	
$50.01 to 99.99	7.00	**Shipping** Shipping and handling must be added. See chart for charges.	
$100 and over	Free	**Gift to Insight for Living Ministries** Tax-deductible in Canada.	

Loomis is also available. Please call for details.

If you are placing an order after January 1, 1997, please call for current prices.

Prices are subject to change without notice.

Total Amount Due Please do not send cash.	$

Payment by: ☐ Cheque or money order payable to Insight for Living Ministries
☐ Credit card

(Circle one): Visa   MasterCard   Number _____

Expiration Date _____   Signature _____

We cannot process your credit card purchase without your signature.

Name _____

Address _____

City _____   Province _____

Postal Code _____   Country _____

Telephone (____) _____   Radio Station ____ ____ ____ ____

If questions arise concerning your order, we may need to contact you.

Mail this order form to the Processing Services Department at the following address:

Insight for Living Ministries
Post Office Box 2510
Vancouver, BC, Canada V6B 3W7

Order Form
United States, Australia, and Other International Locations
(Canadian residents please use order form on reverse side.)

HHTCS represents the entire *Hope in Hurtful Times* series in a special album cover, while HHT 1–9 are the individual tapes included in the series. HHT represents this study guide, should you desire to order additional copies.

HHT	Study guide	$ 4.95 ea.
HHTCS	Cassette series, includes all individual tapes, album cover, and one complimentary study guide	59.50
HHT 1–9	Individual cassettes, includes messages A and B	6.00 ea.

Product Code	Product Description	Quantity	Unit Price	Total
			$	$

			Order Total

Amount of Order	First Class	UPS
$ 7.50 and under	1.00	4.00
$ 7.51 to 12.50	1.50	4.25
$12.51 to 25.00	3.50	4.50
$25.01 to 35.00	4.50	4.75
$35.01 to 60.00	5.50	5.25
$60.00 and over	6.50	5.75

UPS ❑ **First Class** ❑ *Shipping and handling must be added. See chart for charges.*	
Subtotal	
California Residents—Sales Tax *Add 7.25% of subtotal.*	
Non-United States Residents *Australia add 25%. All other locations: U.S. price plus 10% surface postage or 25% airmail.*	
Gift to Insight for Living *Tax-deductible in the United States.*	
Total Amount Due *Please do not send cash.*	$

Fed Ex and Fourth Class are also available. Please call for details.

If you are placing an order after January 1, 1997, please call for current prices.

Prices are subject to change without notice.

Payment by: ❑ Check or money order payable to Insight for Living ❑ Credit card

(Circle one): Visa MasterCard Discover Card American Express BankCard (In Australia)

Number _____

Expiration Date _____ Signature _____

We cannot process your credit card purchase without your signature.

Name _____

Address _____

City _____ State _____

Zip Code _____ Country _____

Telephone (____) _____ Radio Station ____ ____ ____ ____

If questions arise concerning your order, we may need to contact you.

Mail this order form to the Processing Services Department at one of these addresses:

Insight for Living
Post Office Box 69000, Anaheim, CA 92817-0900

Insight for Living, Inc.
GPO Box 2823 EE, Melbourne, VIC 3001, Australia

Order Form
Canadian Residents
(Residents of the United States, Australia, and other international locations, please use order form on reverse side.)

HHTCS represents the entire *Hope in Hurtful Times* series in a special album cover, while HHT 1–9 are the individual tapes included in the series. HHT represents this study guide, should you desire to order additional copies.

HHT	Study guide	$ 6.50 ea.
HHTCS	Cassette series,	69.50
	includes all individual tapes, album cover, and one complimentary study guide	
HHT 1–9	Individual cassettes,	7.48 ea.
	includes messages A and B	

Product Code	Product Description	Quantity	Unit Price	Total
			$	$

Amount of Order	Canada Post
Orders to $10.00	2.00
$10.01 to 30.00	3.50
$30.01 to 50.00	5.00
$50.01 to 99.99	7.00
$100 and over	Free

Loomis is also available. Please call for details.

If you are placing an order after January 1, 1997, please call for current prices.

Prices are subject to change without notice.

Subtotal	
Add 7% GST	
British Columbia Residents *Add 7% sales tax on individual tapes or cassette series.*	
Shipping *Shipping and handling must be added. See chart for charges.*	
Gift to Insight for Living Ministries *Tax-deductible in Canada.*	
Total Amount Due *Please do not send cash.*	$

Payment by: ❏ Cheque or money order payable to Insight for Living Ministries
❏ Credit card

(Circle one): Visa   MasterCard   Number _____

Expiration Date _____   Signature _____
We cannot process your credit card purchase without your signature.

Name _____

Address _____

City _____   Province _____

Postal Code _____   Country _____

Telephone (___) _____   Radio Station ____ ____ ____ ____
If questions arise concerning your order, we may need to contact you.

Mail this order form to the Processing Services Department at the following address:

Insight for Living Ministries
Post Office Box 2510
Vancouver, BC, Canada V6B 3W7

Order Form
United States, Australia, and Other International Locations
(Canadian residents please use order form on reverse side.)

HHTCS represents the entire *Hope in Hurtful Times* series in a special album cover, while HHT 1–9 are the individual tapes included in the series. HHT represents this study guide, should you desire to order additional copies.

HHT	Study guide	**$ 4.95 ea.**
HHTCS	Cassette series,	**59.50**
	includes all individual tapes, album cover, and one complimentary study guide	
HHT 1–9	Individual cassettes,	**6.00 ea.**
	includes messages A and B	

Product Code	Product Description	Quantity	Unit Price	Total
			$	$

			Order Total

Amount of Order	First Class	UPS
$ 7.50 and under	1.00	4.00
$ 7.51 to 12.50	1.50	4.25
$12.51 to 25.00	3.50	4.50
$25.01 to 35.00	4.50	4.75
$35.01 to 60.00	5.50	5.25
$60.00 and over	6.50	5.75

UPS ❏   First Class ❏
Shipping and handling must be added. See chart for charges.

Subtotal

California Residents — Sales Tax
Add 7.25% of subtotal.

Non-United States Residents
Australia add 25%. All other locations: U.S. price plus 10% surface postage or 25% airmail.

Fed Ex and Fourth Class are also available. Please call for details.

Gift to Insight for Living
Tax-deductible in the United States.

If you are placing an order after January 1, 1997, please call for current prices.

Total Amount Due $
Please do not send cash.

Prices are subject to change without notice.

Payment by: ❏ Check or money order payable to Insight for Living   ❏ Credit card

(Circle one):   Visa   MasterCard   Discover Card   American Express   BankCard (In Australia)

Number _____

Expiration Date _____   Signature _____
We cannot process your credit card purchase without your signature.

Name _____

Address _____

City _____   State _____

Zip Code _____   Country _____

Telephone (___) _____   Radio Station ___ ___ ___ ___
If questions arise concerning your order, we may need to contact you.

Mail this order form to the Processing Services Department at one of these addresses:

Insight for Living
Post Office Box 69000, Anaheim, CA 92817-0900

Insight for Living, Inc.
GPO Box 2823 EE, Melbourne, VIC 3001, Australia

Order Form
Canadian Residents
(Residents of the United States, Australia, and other international locations, please use order form on reverse side.)

HHTCS represents the entire *Hope in Hurtful Times* series in a special album cover, while HHT 1–9 are the individual tapes included in the series. HHT represents this study guide, should you desire to order additional copies.

HHT	Study guide	$ 6.50 ea.
HHTCS	Cassette series,	69.50
	includes all individual tapes, album cover, and one complimentary study guide	
HHT 1–9	Individual cassettes,	7.48 ea.
	includes messages A and B	

Product Code	Product Description	Quantity	Unit Price	Total
			$	$

Amount of Order	Canada Post		
Orders to $10.00	2.00
$10.01 to 30.00	3.50
$30.01 to 50.00	5.00
$50.01 to 99.99	7.00
$100 and over	Free

Loomis is also available. Please call for details.

If you are placing an order after January 1, 1997, please call for current prices.

Prices are subject to change without notice.

Subtotal	
Add 7% GST	
British Columbia Residents *Add 7% sales tax on individual tapes or cassette series.*	
Shipping *Shipping and handling must be added. See chart for charges.*	
Gift to Insight for Living Ministries *Tax-deductible in Canada.*	
Total Amount Due *Please do not send cash.*	$

Payment by: ❏ Cheque or money order payable to Insight for Living Ministries
❏ Credit card

(Circle one): Visa   MasterCard   Number _____

Expiration Date _____   Signature _____
We cannot process your credit card purchase without your signature.

Name _____

Address _____

City _____ Province _____

Postal Code _____ Country _____

Telephone (___) _____ Radio Station ____ ____ ____ ____
If questions arise concerning your order, we may need to contact you.

Mail this order form to the Processing Services Department at the following address:

Insight for Living Ministries
Post Office Box 2510
Vancouver, BC, Canada V6B 3W7